Fertility Foods: The Ulti‍mate Cookbook for Hormonal Health and Pregnancy Success

Delicious recipes to boost fertility, balance hormones, and guide your path to parenthood.

Olivia Marindale

Copyright © 2024 by Olivia Marindale
All rights reserved. No part of this publication may be reproduced, stored or transmitted in any form or by any means, electronic, mechanical, photocopying, recording, scanning, or otherwise without written permission from the publisher. It is illegal to copy this book, post it to a website, or distribute it by any other means without permission.
First edition

Table of Contents

1. What This Book Offers
The Connection Between Diet and Fertility

2. Fertility and Nutrition Basics
Understanding Fertility: An Overview of Key Factors for Men and Women
Key Nutrients for Fertility: Nourishing the Body for Conception
Dietary Do's and Don'ts: A Guide for Enhancing Fertility

3. Breakfasts to Kickstart Fertility
1 Fertility Power Smoothie
2 Avocado and Egg Breakfast Bowl
3 Fertility Boost Oatmeal
4 Chia Seed Pudding with Berries
5 Sweet Potato and Black Bean Breakfast Hash
6 Protein-Packed Greek Yogurt Parfait
7 Spinach and Mozzarella Omelette
8 Banana Almond Butter Toast
9 Quinoa Breakfast Bowl with Berries
10 Mango Coconut Smoothie Bowl
11 Blueberry Almond Overnight Oats
12 Sweet Potato Pancakes
13 Cinnamon Apple Quinoa Porridge
14 Pumpkin Spice Fertility Muffins
15 Turmeric Golden Milk Smoothie

4. Lunches Packed with Nutrients
1 Quinoa and Chickpea Power Bowl
2 Salmon and Avocado Salad
3 Lentil and Sweet Potato Stew
4 Mediterranean Chickpea Wrap
5 Avocado Tuna Salad
6 Spinach and Quinoa Stuffed Peppers
7 Fertility-Boosting Buddha Bowl
8 Lentil and Kale Soup
9 Avocado Chicken Salad Wrap
10 Fertility-Boosting Pesto Zoodles
11 Black Bean and Avocado Quinoa Salad
12 Kale and Sweet Potato Salad with Tahini Dressing
13 Grilled Vegetable and Hummus Wrap
14 Lemon Herb Chicken and Farro Salad
15 Eggplant and Chickpea Stew

5. Dinners for Two
1 Lemon Herb Salmon with Asparagus
2 Crispy Ground Beef Stuffed Bell Peppers
3 Garlic Shrimp and Zucchini Noodles
4 Mediterranean Chicken Skillet
5 Butternut Squash and Spinach Risotto
6 Penne Bolognese
7 Baked Cod with Garlic and Herbs
8 Cauliflower Fried Rice with Shrimp
9 Stuffed Portobello Mushrooms with Spinach and Goat Cheese
10 Beef and Broccoli Stir-Fry
11 Chicken and Butternut Squash Sheet Pan Dinner
12 Spicy Chickpea and Spinach Curry
13 Zesty Lemon and Garlic Shrimp Pasta
14 Eggplant Parmesan for Two
15 One-Pan Lemon Herb Chicken and Broccoli
16 Basil Pesto Chicken with Roasted Vegetables
17 Honey Garlic Glazed Salmon
18 Beef and Sweet Potato Skillet
19 Vegetarian Lentil Bolognese
20 Sesame Ginger Tofu Stir-Fry

6. Snacks and Smoothies
1 Fertility Trail Mix
2 Berry Blast Smoothie
3 Pumpkin Seed Energy Bites
4 Avocado Chocolate Smoothie
5 Apple Slices with Almond Butter
6 Green Goddess Smoothie
7 Dark Chocolate and Walnut Bark
8 Berry Chia Pudding
9 Turmeric Golden Milk Smoothie
10 Carrot and Hummus Snack Plate

7. Desserts and Treats
1 Fertility-Boosting Berry Crumble
2 Pomegranate and Dark Chocolate Parfaits
3 Cinnamon-Spiced Pears with Walnuts
4 Chilled Mango and Lime Sorbet
5 Baked Figs with Almond Drizzle
6 Orange and Yogurt Honey Tart
7 Vanilla and Chia Pudding with Passion Fruit
8 Roasted Apple Slices with Cinnamon Yogurt
9 Pineapple Coconut Bliss Bites
10 Avocado and Lime Cheesecake Bars (No-Bake)

8. Supplementing Nutrition with Lifestyle
Lifestyle Factors That Influence Fertility

9. Additional Resources
Tracking Fertility
When to Seek Professional Advice

10. Conclusion

Appendices
Nutrient Index
Frequently Asked Questions
References

Chapter 1 What This Book Offers

This book goes beyond being merely a collection of recipes; it serves as a comprehensive guide to reshaping your relationship with food, particularly in the realm of fertility. As we contemplate the journey into parenthood, it's easy to focus on the significant life changes or medical procedures that lie ahead. However, it's important to recognize the profound influence that food—an integral part of our daily lives—can have on our reproductive health. This book provides you with the essential tools to tap into that power, featuring thoughtfully created recipes that are not only delightful to the palate but also intentionally designed to enhance fertility.

These recipes offer much more than just basic nutritional guidance. These are grounded in the most recent scientific findings that link particular nutrients to reproductive health, taking into account factors such as hormonal balance, cell vitality, and energy levels. This book features recipes thoughtfully designed to nourish your body with the essential blend of vitamins, minerals, healthy fats, and antioxidants, all of which are essential for supporting fertility. This approach goes beyond strict dieting; it focuses on creating meaningful daily meals and selecting ingredients that support the body's natural ability to conceive.

Nourishing the Body at Every Meal

Food has long been regarded as the original medicine. The ingredients we consume play a crucial role in influencing every cell, system, and process within our bodies, including those related to reproduction. This book truly embraces the idea of enhancing fertility by highlighting foods that are rich in nutrients and possess beneficial properties. Every meal in this book is carefully crafted to deliver the vital nutrients necessary for fostering a supportive environment for fertility.

Beginning with breakfast, you'll discover recipes that feature nutrient-rich ingredients designed to kickstart your day on a positive note. Breakfast recipes can feature fertility-friendly choices such as antioxidant-rich berries, high-fiber oats, and protein-packed nuts and seeds. These ingredients do more than just satisfy your hunger; they are thoughtfully selected to offer your body lasting energy, help maintain stable blood sugar levels, and support healthy insulin regulation—essential elements for achieving hormonal balance and promoting reproductive health. Numerous breakfast recipes incorporate healthy fats, essential for hormone production and beneficial for brain function.

This book's lunches are designed to provide lasting energy throughout the afternoon while thoughtfully incorporating essential nutrients such as folate, iron, and zinc. Discover a variety of recipes that feature leafy greens, legumes, and lean proteins. These ingredients come together to promote egg and sperm health, assist in cellular repair, and create a nurturing environment for the uterus. This book presents an array of lunch choices, ranging from colorful salads to satisfying soups, designed to accommodate diverse tastes and dietary requirements, all while supporting your body's needs for optimal reproductive health.

Dinner recipes are designed to unite partners around meals that not only fulfill hunger but also deeply nourish the body. These dishes showcase foods that support fertility, such as salmon, which is abundant in omega-3 fatty acids that help reduce inflammation and promote hormone production. Additionally, roasted vegetables are filled with fiber and antioxidants, contributing to detoxification and gut health. Dinner transforms into a precious moment to relax, strengthen bonds, and nourish your body with the essential nutrients that foster a supportive environment for conception.

The Impact of Thoughtful Ingredients

Every ingredient in these recipes is selected thoughtfully and with intention. A simple handful of spinach is more than just a leafy green; it's a remarkable source of folate, a vital B-vitamin that plays a crucial role in the synthesis and repair of DNA in reproductive cells. Eggs are more than just a breakfast favorite; they are rich in choline, a vital nutrient that supports fetal brain development and cellular health for both partners. These recipes help you select and blend foods to enhance their benefits, transforming each ingredient into a supportive partner on your journey to fertility.

This book highlights how critical it is to use quality ingredients. Whenever possible, recipes recommend using organic products to help minimize exposure to pesticides, as these substances can disrupt hormone function. Choosing grass-fed, pasture-raised meats and organic dairy products is a wise decision, as they offer enhanced nutrient profiles and are free from synthetic hormones that can interfere with your body's natural hormonal balance. When you choose your ingredients thoughtfully, you're giving your body the pure, nutrient-rich fuel it requires to perform at its peak.

Supporting Hormonal Balance and Reducing Inflammation

This book features a variety of recipes thoughtfully crafted to support hormonal balance. Incorporating healthy fats from sources such as avocado, olive oil, and nuts can play a vital role in supporting the production of reproductive hormones. In contrast to trans fats and highly processed oils, these fats play an important role in reducing inflammation, which is essential for supporting fertility. Chronic inflammation can disrupt ovulation and affect sperm health, which is why these recipes are thoughtfully crafted with a variety of anti-inflammatory ingredients to help promote a more balanced internal environment.

Inflammation can be a significant challenge for couples on their journey to conceive, and adjusting your diet can be one of the most impactful strategies to address it. Incorporating foods such as fatty fish, berries, leafy greens, and nuts into your meals can create a consistent and natural way to help reduce inflammation in your body. Every meal serves as a meaningful step towards restoring balance, benefiting not only fertility but also enhancing overall health.

Recipes that Rejuvenate: Antioxidant Powerhouses

Oxidative stress arises when there are more free radicals in the body than it can effectively neutralize, and it is recognized as a significant factor in infertility. It harms cells, including both egg and sperm cells, which can impact their quality and viability. Antioxidants help fight oxidative stress by neutralizing free radicals, which safeguard reproductive cells from premature aging and damage. This book offers a collection of recipes that are abundant in antioxidants, ensuring your body receives a consistent supply of these beneficial compounds.

Berries are truly remarkable, and often celebrated for their potent antioxidant properties. You'll find them gracing breakfast bowls, enriching smoothies, and adding a delightful touch to desserts. Incorporating dark leafy greens such as kale and spinach, along with vibrant vegetables like tomatoes, bell peppers, and carrots, can truly enhance your lunch and dinner recipes. These foods do more than brighten your plate; they play a vital role in protecting and rejuvenating your cells, helping to safeguard your body's reproductive tissues from potential harm.

Building a Sustainable Fertility-Boosting Lifestyle

Eating well is fundamental, and it's just as important that the recipes in this book integrate effortlessly into your everyday routine. The recipes are designed to be straightforward and practical, recognizing that the path to fertility should be a fulfilling experience rather than a burden. No matter if you're preparing a meal for yourself or sharing it with someone special, these recipes are thoughtfully crafted to accommodate your hectic lifestyle while ensuring you receive the utmost nourishment. Discover recipes that are perfect for prepping ahead of time, designed to be made in larger batches for those delightful leftovers, or easily modified to suit different cooking skill levels.

The aim extends beyond merely enhancing fertility in the immediate future; it's about establishing a solid foundation for a lifelong commitment to overall wellness. These recipes offer a wonderful opportunity to cultivate sustainable habits that nourish the body, transforming the fertility journey into one of enrichment rather than restrictions. With each meal, you are nurturing your body's ability to foster life, establishing a daily routine that enhances your reproductive health for the long term.

Recipes for Two: Deepening Connections Through Shared Meals

This book stands out with its emphasis on recipes that bring partners together, nurturing connection while pursuing a common goal. Research indicates that sharing meals can enhance relationships, and when it comes to a fertility journey, nurturing this connection is especially vital. When both partners prioritize their nutrition and align their dietary choices, they foster a nurturing atmosphere that benefits not only the journey of conception but also strengthens their relationship as a whole.

Many of the dinner recipes are thoughtfully designed for couples, ensuring that you both can enjoy the benefits of fertility-supportive ingredients. Imagine enjoying a warm, inviting evening meal featuring wild-caught salmon alongside perfectly roasted root vegetables, or savoring a hearty lentil and vegetable stew brimming with fiber, protein, and vital nutrients. These meals provide nourishment that extends beyond the physical; they foster moments of connection and a shared dedication to the journey you both embrace.

More Than Just Recipes: Support and Useful Advice

This book goes beyond just recipes. This resource offers valuable insights on how to approach grocery shopping with fertility in mind, including helpful tips for reading labels and effective strategies for dining out while keeping your health a top priority. This resource includes helpful sections on meal prepping for those hectic weeks, tips for optimizing your pantry with fertility-supportive staples, and thoughtful guidance on managing food cravings and indulgences while staying on course.

Food holds a special place in our hearts, and we understand that the path to fertility can be filled with a range of emotions. This book honors that journey, providing much more than a simple compilation of ingredients and instructions. The goal is to equip you with the knowledge, inspiration, and confidence needed to make choices that lead you closer to your aspirations.

A Warm Welcome to Your Journey of Parenthood

This book warmly invites you to discover how food can play a meaningful role in your fertility journey. Every recipe is thoughtfully designed, not merely to satisfy your hunger but to nurture your aspiration of building a family. The journey to parenthood can be tough, yet with each meal, you're making significant strides toward a future brimming with hope, health, and vitality.

These recipes can be more than just meals; they represent moments of nourishment, resilience, and joy. By embracing these choices, you are nurturing your body and laying a strong foundation for the journey that lies ahead. Each delicious bite contributes to a space where fertility can thrive naturally.

The Connection Between Diet and Fertility

Embarking on the journey to parenthood is a unique adventure, brimming with hopes, hurdles, and plenty of curiosity about how to boost the chances of conception. One of the most influential and frequently overlooked parts of this journey is diet. Nutrition not only powers our bodies; it shapes them too! The reproductive system, with its intricate dance of hormones and cells, thrives on certain nutrients, making diet an effective way to boost fertility!

Fertility Starts with Cellular Health

At the core of fertility is a profound reality: each path to conception starts at the cellular level. Our bodies, made up of trillions of cells, depend on each one to operate with accuracy and energy. In the realm of reproductive health, the sperm and egg—essential components of life—need to be at their best to foster the possibility of a new beginning. Cellular health is not something that occurs by chance; it is significantly shaped by the choices we make regarding what we consume daily.

Picture each cell as a small factory, tirelessly engaged in its own unique tasks. The journey of reproductive cells is truly remarkable: the egg undergoes a maturation process, preparing itself for the moment of fertilization, while sperm exhibit incredible resilience, speed, and agility as they strive to reach and penetrate the egg. The efficiency of these factories relies heavily on the nutrients they receive. When these essential elements are lacking, production can slow down, quality may suffer, and the journey to conception can become increasingly difficult.

Consider folate, a vital B-vitamin that helps in the synthesis and repair of DNA. This nutrient, often present in leafy greens, beans, and fortified grains, serves as a protective barrier for the genetic material within each cell. Folate plays a key role for women by helping to ensure that the DNA of the egg is intact and prepared to unite with sperm, paving the way for the development of a healthy embryo. For men, it plays a crucial role in maintaining sperm DNA integrity, which helps lower the risk of genetic mutations that might affect fertility or result in complications.

Omega-3 fatty acids are equally important. Healthy fats found in foods such as salmon, flaxseeds, and walnuts are not only beneficial for heart health, but they help maintain cellular flexibility. Sperm embarks on a remarkable journey, one that requires both resilience and adaptability. Omega-3s serve a critical role in creating a flexible and resilient cell membrane, which facilitates the smooth movement of sperm. When these fats are lacking, sperm can face challenges, and their motility—an essential element for successful conception—may be compromised.

Zinc is essential in supporting cellular health, particularly when it comes to fertility. It can be found in foods such as pumpkin seeds, chickpeas, and shellfish, benefiting both men and women alike. Zinc supports men in producing high-quality sperm. It ensures that sperm are well-formed and have a healthy head and tail structure, enabling them to effectively reach the egg. Zinc is essential for women, particularly in supporting cell division during the critical early stages of embryo development. When zinc levels drop, it can lead to irregular cell division, which may impact the viability of the embryo.

Cellular health is not just about individual nutrients; it's a harmonious interplay of various vitamins, minerals, and antioxidants working together. Vitamin C plays a crucial role alongside zinc in enhancing sperm quality. Vitamin C serves as a powerful antioxidant, protecting reproductive cells from oxidative stress, which can lead to premature cell breakdown. Oxidative stress can arise from various factors, including an unhealthy diet, high levels of stress, or exposure to environmental toxins. When left unchecked, cells, particularly the delicate sperm and egg cells, face a significant risk of damage. Incorporating antioxidant-rich foods such as berries, bell peppers, and citrus fruits into your diet can be a wonderful way to support your body. These foods help create a protective shield, preserving cellular integrity and enhancing fertility.

For women, an important nutrient to consider is vitamin D. Vitamin D is often recognized for its importance in maintaining bone health, but it also supports ovarian function. A nurturing ovarian environment has a significant role in fostering the growth of healthy eggs, preparing them for the important moment of ovulation. Vitamin D helps regulate this process, ensuring that eggs remain healthy and mature in harmony with the body's hormonal cycles.

The nutrients collaborate seamlessly, forming a supportive network that empowers each cell and boosts its overall function. Every meal we choose has an essential part in our cellular health, which in turn influences our reproductive health. Each bite can either enhance your fertility journey or create obstacles along the way. By prioritizing nutrient-dense foods, we are nurturing the essential building blocks of our fertility—the very cells that hold the potential for life.

The Hormonal Symphony and Diet's Influence

The body's hormonal system resembles a symphony orchestra, where each hormone acts as an instrument contributing to a seamless and harmonious melody. In the realm of fertility, these hormones collaborate in a beautifully orchestrated manner, directing essential processes such as ovulation, sperm production, and the body's readiness for pregnancy. When all aspects are in harmony, the body resonates with vitality, prepared and receptive to the potential of new beginnings. When even a single note in this symphony goes out of tune, it can impact the whole performance. Diet, frequently underestimated, serves as a vital conductor that ensures this hormonal orchestra performs in perfect harmony.

Hormones serve as vital chemical messengers, transmitting important signals between various organs and systems in the body. In the process of reproduction, several key hormones play key roles. Estrogen, progesterone, testosterone, and luteinizing hormone each contribute uniquely to preparing the body for conception. Estrogen assists in thickening the uterine lining, creating a nurturing environment for a fertilized egg, while progesterone is essential for supporting a pregnancy should conception take place. Testosterone is commonly linked to men, but it plays a crucial role for women as well. It affects libido and contributes to maintaining muscle and bone strength, which are vital for overall reproductive health.

The impact of diet on these hormones is significant. Fats are critical for hormone production, serving as the foundational building blocks for the synthesis of many reproductive hormones. Healthy fats, such as those in avocados, olive oil, nuts, and fatty fish, are essential as they supply cholesterol, which is a crucial building block for hormones like estrogen, progesterone, and testosterone. When the body is deficient in these essential fats, it can hinder hormone production, resulting in irregular cycles, decreased libido, or other challenges that may affect the journey to conception.

It's important to recognize that not all fats impact hormonal balance in the same way. Trans fats, commonly present in processed foods and fried snacks, can significantly disrupt this delicate hormonal balance. These factors can contribute to heightened inflammation, disrupt insulin levels, and result in hormonal resistance, which makes it challenging for the body to effectively respond to its own hormonal signals. For women, this can interfere with ovulation, and for men, it may reduce testosterone levels, which can directly affect sperm quality and libido. The effect resembles a discordant note in an otherwise flawless symphony, interrupting the delicate balance essential for conception.

Carbohydrates are also important in this intricate hormonal interplay, especially when it comes to regulating insulin. This hormone, often linked to blood sugar management, also has a profound impact on reproductive health. Consuming a diet rich in refined sugars and processed carbohydrates can trigger insulin spikes, which may result in hormonal imbalances in the body. The body responds by producing additional insulin to handle these sugars, which can disrupt the delicate balance of other hormones, especially in women. Elevated insulin levels can contribute to conditions such as polycystic ovary syndrome

(PCOS), which is a prevalent factor in infertility. This condition is often associated with irregular menstrual cycles and the absence of ovulation.

To create a balance, incorporating complex carbohydrates such as whole grains, vegetables, and legumes can offer a consistent and gradual source of energy to keep insulin levels stable. This consistency helps to avoid hormonal fluctuations, enabling the body to remain in harmony with its natural reproductive cycles. Maintaining balanced insulin levels is key for men, as it plays a significant role in supporting testosterone production, which in turn contributes to a healthy libido and sperm quality.

In addition to fats and carbs, some micronutrients play a subtle but vital role in this intricate hormonal balance.
Magnesium, commonly present in dark leafy greens, nuts, and seeds, helps manage the stress hormone cortisol. Elevated stress and cortisol levels can disrupt reproductive hormones, leading to irregular cycles and reduced testosterone levels in men. Magnesium has a vital role in supporting cortisol regulation and helps ensure that stress does not overshadow the other important elements of our hormonal symphony.

Phytoestrogens are natural compounds present in foods such as soy, flaxseed, and legumes, contributing to the intricate balance of hormones in our bodies. Plant-based estrogens have the ability to either mimic or adjust the body's natural estrogen levels. Women experiencing low estrogen levels may find that phytoestrogens offer gentle support for their hormonal balance, aiding in the maintenance of the uterine lining and promoting regular menstrual cycles. Women experiencing high estrogen levels may find relief by occupying receptor sites, which can help balance the overall effects of estrogen in the body. This adaptability makes phytoestrogens especially valuable, functioning like a versatile instrument that adjusts its tone according to the needs of the performance.

For men, achieving hormonal harmony is crucial, as balanced testosterone levels play a vital role in various aspects of health, including sperm production, energy levels, and mood stability. As we age, it's natural for testosterone levels to decrease, but making mindful dietary choices can play a significant role in slowing this process. Nutrients such as vitamin D, are important for maintaining healthy testosterone levels. Men who have low vitamin D levels frequently face challenges with low testosterone, which can affect their fertility and libido. Incorporating a diet that includes vitamin D, lean proteins, and healthy fats can assist in maintaining healthy testosterone levels.

The last element of the hormonal puzzle is all about when we eat our meals. The body's hormonal rhythms are intricately connected to the circadian rhythm, which serves as our natural 24-hour biological clock. Having regular meal times can truly support your body's natural rhythm. It provides consistent energy sources, which helps to minimize unnecessary hormonal stress. When we skip meals or indulge in binge eating, it can throw our bodies off balance. This disruption can place stress on the adrenal glands, resulting in cortisol spikes that may interfere with our reproductive hormones. Maintaining a balanced and regular eating schedule helps to support the body's natural timing, ensuring that every aspect of our hormonal symphony stays in harmony.

Diet transcends being merely a source of fuel; it serves as the conductor of the body's reproductive harmony, orchestrating each hormone to fulfill its role. By nourishing ourselves with balanced meals that include the right fats, proteins, carbs, and micronutrients, we're not only supporting our health but also fostering an environment where hormones can interact harmoniously, fertility can thrive, and the body can function together toward the beautiful possibility of new life. The beauty of a symphony comes from the harmonious collaboration of each instrument, much like how reproductive health is attained through the precise balance and timing of every hormone involved. By making thoughtful dietary choices, we take on the roles of both audience and conductor, creating a setting for a performance that can lead to truly remarkable results.

Inflammation: The Hidden Barrier to Fertility

Inflammation can be a subtle adversary when it comes to fertility, often hiding in the background and quietly affecting various aspects such as hormonal balance and cellular health. When we consider inflammation, it often brings to mind the body's quick reaction to a small injury—like a swollen finger from a paper cut or a sensitive spot around a bruise. Chronic inflammation is a subtle yet persistent issue, quietly affecting our bodies over weeks, months, or even years. It creates an environment that can disturb the fragile balance essential for conception.

This concealed challenge emerges from numerous origins, many of which are closely linked to the choices we make every day, particularly regarding our diet. Foods that are high in processed sugars, trans fats, and refined carbohydrates can keep the immune system in a state of constant alert. In moderation, these foods may not pose a risk, but when they become central to our diet, our bodies can remain in a constant state of alert, leading to the release of inflammatory molecules throughout our system.

The ongoing presence of low-grade inflammation can significantly affect fertility. For women, this can result in challenges with ovulation, as inflammation disrupts the communication between the brain and the ovaries. The brain's signals for releasing essential hormones can become confused, leading to irregular ovulation or even preventing it entirely. This disruption can trigger a series of events that impact the entire reproductive system, hindering its ability to function in harmony.

For men, the narrative remains quite similar. Inflammation can impact testosterone production and sperm quality, which may hinder the ability of sperm to reach and fertilize an egg. Oxidative stress can occur, which involves free radicals causing damage to cells, including the sensitive structures of sperm and eggs. Picture sperm cells as small swimmers, each requiring the strength and guidance to find their way to their goal. Chronic inflammation can feel like a persistent force, steering these swimmers off their intended path and diminishing their stamina.

Anti-inflammatory foods, on the other hand, help to soothe this internal unrest. They provide a protective barrier, strengthening the body's natural defenses and enabling the immune system to feel at ease. By enjoying foods packed with antioxidants, such as blueberries, leafy greens, and nuts, we're not just taking care of our bodies; we're also playing a crucial role in combating free radicals that can harm our cells. Berries are a wonderful source of vitamins C and E, which have a major role in fighting oxidative stress and safeguarding reproductive cells. Incorporating these foods into our diet empowers our bodies to combat internal wear and tear, helping to maintain the quality of eggs and sperm.

Olive oil, a beloved component of the Mediterranean diet, serves as a remarkable ally in combating inflammation. It includes oleic acid, a type of monounsaturated fat that has demonstrated the ability to lower inflammation markers in the body. Incorporating it into your daily meals—maybe by drizzling it over salads or using it in your cooking—can serve as a gentle, consistent support for regulating immune responses. Fatty fish such as salmon, mackerel, and sardines are not only delicious but also packed with omega-3 fatty acids. These nutrients reduce inflammation by influencing the production of inflammatory molecules, making them essential for anyone looking to enhance their fertility through diet.

The Connection Between Gut Health and Fertility

The link between gut health and fertility might not seem clear at first, but recent studies show that the gut goes beyond digestion; it significantly impacts reproductive health. Imagine the gut as a vibrant city teeming with microorganisms—trillions of bacteria, fungi, and other microbes, all collaborating in a beautifully balanced ecosystem called the microbiome. A balanced ecosystem is essential for our overall health, influencing everything from immune function to hormone regulation, and it even plays an essential role in preparing the body for conception.

Picture the gut as a skilled conductor leading an orchestra, making sure that every note—the nutrients we take in, the hormones we create, the messages sent to our immune system—remains in perfect harmony. When this balance is disrupted by factors such as a poor diet, stress, or environmental influences, the harmony can be affected, potentially leading to challenges with fertility.

The gut has a key role in absorbing nutrients. Each meal we enjoy travels through the gut, where vital vitamins and minerals are carefully extracted and distributed to various parts of our body. When the gut is out of balance, it can have a hard time absorbing essential nutrients, which means the body may not get the vital resources it requires for healthy reproductive function. The absence of these essential nutrients can significantly impact the body's capacity to produce healthy eggs and sperm. This deficiency may lead to fluctuations in hormone production, which can disrupt the menstrual cycle and influence sperm count and motility.

In addition to its role in nutrient absorption, the gut plays a significant part in managing inflammation, which is essential for maintaining reproductive health. A thriving gut microbiome generates compounds that soothe inflammation, creating a nurturing environment for reproduction. When the gut microbiome is compromised, it can lead to inflammation, creating a challenging environment for both sperm and eggs. A well-balanced gut plays a crucial role in lowering these barriers, which can enhance the likelihood of conception.

The gut helps regulate excess hormones, particularly estrogen, by effectively breaking it down and eliminating it from the body. Incorporating fiber-rich foods like leafy greens, legumes, and whole grains into your diet can significantly support your body's natural processes by binding to excess estrogen and aiding in its elimination. Maintaining gut health goes beyond just avoiding discomfort; it plays a crucial role in actively supporting hormonal balance.

Probiotics, the friendly bacteria present in fermented foods such as yogurt, kefir, sauerkraut, and miso, are essential for maintaining a healthy gut balance. They fill the gut with beneficial bacteria that improve digestion, fight off harmful bacteria, and bolster the immune system. Incorporating these foods into a fertility-focused diet can play a significant role in restoring and maintaining a healthy gut microbiome, ultimately fostering a more supportive environment for conception. In addition to probiotics, incorporating prebiotic foods such as garlic, onions, and asparagus can significantly support the growth of these beneficial bacteria, providing them with the essential fuel they require to flourish.

Building Fertility-Boosting Habits

Staying consistent is essential for any dietary change, particularly in the context of enhancing fertility. Although enjoying a single nutrient-rich meal can be beneficial, it's the consistent accumulation of these healthy choices over time that truly influences reproductive health in a significant way. Just like our bodies are constantly renewing cells, making thoughtful daily dietary choices fosters a healthier cellular environment that supports and enhances fertility.

For individuals and couples looking to conceive, embracing a mindset focused on gradual, sustainable changes can be more beneficial than seeking quick fixes. Even in the face of challenges, maintaining a fertility-friendly diet can help the body move closer to its ideal state for conception. Food serves as more than just fuel; it is a vital partner in crafting our future.

Chapter 2 Fertility and Nutrition Basics

Understanding Fertility: An Overview of Key Factors for Men and Women

Fertility is a complex and intricate system that depends on the harmonious functioning of various biological processes in both men and women. Fertility is often viewed as a straightforward idea—you're either fertile or you're not. However, the truth is much more complex. It's shaped by a variety of factors that interact to establish the right conditions for conception. By grasping these internal and external factors, individuals and couples can feel empowered to actively enhance their fertility journey.

In this subchapter, we will delve into the essential factors influencing fertility in both men and women. We aim to illuminate how the body's natural processes intertwine with lifestyle choices, genetics, and environmental influences. By exploring the factors that influence fertility, we can empower ourselves to make informed choices that promote reproductive health.

Female Fertility: A Delicate Balancing Act

Female fertility is truly a remarkable aspect of biology—a sophisticated process that unfolds with grace and precision, month after month, as the body readies itself for the potential of bringing new life into the world. This delicate balancing act is much more complex than it might seem at first glance. Fertility goes beyond just having a regular menstrual cycle; it is shaped by a complex interplay of various factors, all of which play a crucial role in the body's capacity to conceive and maintain a pregnancy. Grasping these factors allows women and their partners to appreciate the subtlety and accuracy needed to attain the best possible fertility outcomes.

The menstrual cycle, a process that spans approximately 28 days, is central to female fertility. It orchestrates the maturation of an egg and readies the body for the possibility of pregnancy. The cycle is influenced by a sophisticated interaction of hormones that serve as chemical messengers, guiding the body's reproductive system. Every month, a woman's ovaries get ready to release eggs, while her uterus creates a supportive environment for a fertilized egg to settle in. It's a beautiful interplay of biological processes, and when all elements are harmonized, conception can take place. When any part of this system struggles, it can throw the whole process off balance.

The journey of fertility starts in the ovaries, where a woman is born with all the eggs she will ever possess. In contrast to men, who have a continuous production of sperm throughout their lives, women have a limited supply of eggs that decreases as they age. At the time of birth, a female baby is born with around one to two million eggs. As puberty approaches, the number of eggs a girl has decreased to approximately 300,000 to 400,000. By her mid-thirties, both the quantity and quality of her eggs start to decline at a faster pace. This decline doesn't indicate that conception is out of reach; rather, it suggests that the opportunity for fertility starts to become more limited.

At the start of each menstrual cycle, a group of eggs begins to develop, yet usually, only one egg reaches full maturity and is released during ovulation. The process is influenced by hormones, mainly estrogen and progesterone, which help regulate the growth and release of the egg, while also preparing the uterus to welcome a fertilized egg. Estrogen, which is produced by the developing follicles in the ovaries, plays a crucial role in thickening the uterine lining. This process creates a nutrient-rich environment that is essential for an embryo to implant and grow successfully. When estrogen levels drop too low, it can hinder the proper development of the uterine lining, which may pose challenges for an embryo to successfully implant, despite the occurrence of fertilization.

Ovulation marks the moment when a mature egg is released from the ovary, representing the peak of the first half of the menstrual cycle. The process is initiated by an increase in luteinizing hormone (LH), which the pituitary gland releases as a reaction to elevated estrogen levels. The intricate balance of hormones plays a vital role in ensuring that the egg is released at just the right moment. When the delicate balance of hormones is disrupted—due to stress, illness, or lifestyle choices—ovulation can be delayed or may not happen at all, which can make conception challenging for that month.

However, ovulation marks only the start of the journey. After the egg is released, it journeys down the fallopian tube, where it has the opportunity to meet sperm and potentially become fertilized. When fertilization takes place, the newly formed embryo embarks on its journey to the uterus, where it will strive to implant itself in the thickened uterine lining. At this point, progesterone plays a crucial role, ensuring the uterine lining is preserved and providing essential support during the early stages of pregnancy. Progesterone, often referred to as the "pregnancy hormone," helps establish a stable environment that supports the development of an embryo. When progesterone levels are insufficient, a fertilized egg can face challenges in both implantation and maintaining its position, which may result in early pregnancy loss.

Hormonal balance is a dynamic process, shaped by a variety of internal and external factors that can change over time. Stress can significantly impact a woman's hormonal balance. During times of elevated stress, the body responds by releasing cortisol, which can disrupt the regular production of reproductive hormones such as estrogen and progesterone. Chronic stress can sometimes result in anovulation, a situation where ovulation does not take place at all. The body prioritizes survival over reproduction, viewing high stress as a significant threat to overall well-being.

Conditions such as polycystic ovary syndrome (PCOS) add another layer of complexity to the situation. PCOS stands as one of the leading contributors to infertility in women, marked by hormonal imbalances, especially the overproduction of androgens, which are male hormones. Hormonal imbalances can significantly affect the normal maturation of eggs, which may result in irregular or even absent ovulation. Women experiencing PCOS often face challenges such as irregular periods, trouble predicting ovulation, and, in certain instances, anovulatory cycles, where an egg is not released. Effectively managing PCOS involves making thoughtful lifestyle changes, including maintaining a healthy weight, incorporating regular exercise, and adjusting your diet. These steps can significantly aid in regulating insulin levels and achieving hormonal balance.

One important aspect that frequently gets overlooked is the condition of the fallopian tubes. The narrow tubes have a critical role in fertility, acting as the vital pathway for the egg's journey from the ovary to the uterus. When fallopian tubes are blocked or damaged, it can create a barrier that prevents the egg and sperm from coming together, which means fertilization cannot occur. Conditions such as endometriosis, pelvic inflammatory disease (PID), and sexually transmitted infections (STIs) can lead to scarring or blockages in the fallopian tubes, which may decrease the likelihood of achieving natural conception. Recognizing and addressing these conditions early is essential for preserving fertility, as any irreversible harm to the fallopian tubes can greatly impact the likelihood of conception.

In addition to hormonal and physical factors, age plays a key role in influencing female fertility. As women grow older, the quality of their eggs can diminish, which may lead to a higher risk of chromosomal abnormalities and a lower likelihood of successful fertilization. After the age of 35, it's common to notice a more significant decline in both the quality and quantity of eggs. This is an important aspect to consider during this stage of life. Advancements in fertility treatments, like in vitro fertilization (IVF), have opened new doors for women to conceive later in life. However, it's important to recognize that age continues to be a significant factor in natural conception. For women looking to safeguard their fertility, egg freezing has emerged as a valuable choice, enabling them to preserve their eggs for potential future use.

The uterine environment plays a vital role in female fertility. A robust and healthy uterine lining ensures successful implantation. Following ovulation, the increase in progesterone plays a crucial role in thickening the uterine lining, enhancing its ability to welcome a fertilized egg. When the uterine lining is too thin or affected by hormonal imbalances or medical conditions, it can hinder implantation, even if fertilization has successfully occurred. This underscores the significance of maintaining hormonal balance not just in the first half of the menstrual cycle, but throughout the entire cycle.

Lifestyle factors significantly influence female fertility. It's important to recognize that maintaining a healthy body weight matters for women's health, as both underweight and overweight individuals may face challenges with their menstrual cycles. When someone is underweight, their body may respond by conserving energy, which can lead to a suppression of ovulation. This is a protective mechanism to help the body manage the potential stress of pregnancy. Conversely, carrying excess weight, especially around the midsection, can disrupt hormonal balance and impact ovulation. Maintaining a healthy weight, engaging in regular physical activity, and following a nutrient-dense diet can significantly enhance overall fertility and foster a more harmonious hormonal balance.

The intricacies of female fertility represent a dynamic system that relies on a careful balance of hormones, organ health, and lifestyle factors. The menstrual cycle serves as a clear indicator of fertility, yet the intricate processes that drive it are always changing, influenced by a variety of internal and external factors. Grasping this intricate balancing act enables women to take charge of their reproductive health, allowing them to make informed choices that nurture their fertility, whether they are currently trying to conceive or looking to preserve their fertility for the future.

Male Fertility: A Numbers Game of Quality and Quantity

Male fertility often flies under the radar, especially in comparison to the intense focus placed on female fertility. But make no mistake: male fertility is just as important, and it hinges on a delicate interplay between quality and quantity. Fertility for men comes down to more than simply having a sperm count within the "normal" range. The health and ability of sperm to reach, penetrate, and fertilize an egg are equally as important as how many sperm are present. It's a nuanced process, and for those hoping to conceive, understanding the balance between sperm quality and quantity can be the key to unlocking fertility success.

At the core of male fertility is sperm production. Unlike women, who are born with a finite number of eggs, men continuously produce sperm throughout their lives. The process of sperm production—called spermatogenesis—happens within the testes and takes about 64 days from start to finish. During this time, the testes create millions of sperm cells daily. However, while men produce an enormous number of sperm, only a fraction of these are viable candidates for fertilizing an egg. It's truly a game of numbers—more sperm increases the chances of conception, but even with high sperm counts, only a few are capable of completing the journey to fertilization.

Healthy sperm count is a starting point in this numbers game, with anything over 15 million sperm per milliliter of semen considered within the normal range. But having a high sperm count doesn't guarantee success. In fact, the quality of those sperm is often the more critical factor when it comes to conception. A high count may flood the reproductive system with millions of sperm, but if those sperm are weak, slow, or misshapen, their odds of fertilizing an egg plummet. It's like fielding a sports team: sheer numbers don't matter if the players aren't fit for the game.

One of the most essential factors in sperm quality is motility—the ability of sperm to swim. To reach an egg, sperm must embark on a journey through the female reproductive system, navigating the cervix, uterus, and fallopian tubes. This journey is long and arduous for such microscopic swimmers, and it requires energy and agility. Sperm motility is measured in terms of how many sperm are actively moving forward in a straight line, which is fundamental for them to reach the egg. Poor motility can result in sperm falling short of their target, leaving even a healthy sperm count ineffective.

Morphology, or the shape and structure of sperm, is another significant aspect of quality. Healthy sperm have an oval head, a midsection packed with energy-producing mitochondria, and a long tail that propels them forward. However, many sperm have defects—heads that are too large or too small, misshapen tails, or other abnormalities that affect their ability to swim effectively or penetrate an egg. A man may have a large number of sperm, but if a significant portion of them have poor morphology, conception may still be difficult.

The factors that influence sperm quality and quantity are varied, with both internal and external elements playing a role. Testosterone, often seen as the hormone of masculinity, is central to sperm production. Testosterone drives the creation of sperm cells, and men with low testosterone levels may experience a decline in sperm production. While testosterone naturally declines with age, lifestyle factors such as poor diet, lack of exercise, and high stress levels can exacerbate this decline, making it more difficult to maintain healthy sperm production.

But testosterone alone isn't enough to support fertility. Other hormones, such as follicle-stimulating hormone (FSH) and luteinizing hormone (LH), also play vital roles in sperm production. FSH stimulates the testes to produce sperm, while LH triggers the production of testosterone. Any imbalance in these hormones can disrupt sperm production, leading to lower sperm counts or reduced sperm quality. Hormonal imbalances may arise from stress, obesity, or certain medical conditions, but they can often be addressed through lifestyle changes and medical intervention.

Environmental factors also heavily influence sperm health. Heat, for instance, is a major concern when it comes to male fertility. The testes are located outside of the body for a reason—they need to stay cooler than the rest of the body to produce healthy sperm. Exposure to high temperatures, whether from hot tubs, saunas, tight clothing, or even prolonged sitting with laptops on the lap, can temporarily reduce sperm count by impairing spermatogenesis. While the effects of heat are usually reversible, consistent exposure can have long-term consequences on sperm production.

Beyond heat, exposure to environmental toxins such as pesticides, heavy metals, and industrial chemicals can wreak havoc on sperm health. These toxins can cause oxidative stress, a condition in which harmful molecules called free radicals damage sperm cells. Oxidative stress leads to DNA fragmentation in sperm, making them less capable of fertilizing an egg or increasing the risk of genetic abnormalities in the offspring. Avoiding exposure to harmful chemicals, adopting healthy eating habits, and incorporating antioxidants into the diet can help mitigate the effects of oxidative stress and improve sperm quality.

Diet is another cornerstone of male fertility. Just as the body requires proper nutrition to function, sperm production is highly dependent on the availability of key nutrients. Zinc, for example, is critical for testosterone production and sperm health. Found in foods like oysters, pumpkin seeds, and lean meats, zinc helps maintain sperm count, motility, and morphology. Low zinc levels can lead to reduced testosterone, poorer sperm quality, and lower chances of conception.

Vitamin C is another nutrient that plays an essential role in male fertility. As a powerful antioxidant, vitamin C helps protect sperm from oxidative stress, which can damage their DNA and impair their function. Consuming foods rich in vitamin C, such as citrus fruits, bell peppers, and broccoli, can reduce DNA fragmentation in sperm, improving their chances of successfully fertilizing an egg. Similarly, omega-3 fatty acids—found in fatty fish like salmon, flaxseeds, and walnuts—help support sperm membrane integrity, making sperm more resilient and capable of completing their journey to the egg.

Exercise, too, has a profound effect on sperm health. Regular physical activity helps maintain a healthy weight, reduces stress, and boosts testosterone levels—all factors that improve sperm quality. However, moderation is key. Excessive exercise, particularly endurance activities that push the body to extremes, can have the opposite effect, reducing testosterone levels and impairing sperm production. Striking a balance between staying active and avoiding overexertion helps create an optimal environment for sperm production.

Stress is often underestimated in its impact on male fertility. Chronic stress can lead to elevated cortisol levels, which interfere with testosterone production and disrupt the delicate hormonal balance needed for healthy sperm production. Stress management techniques such as mindfulness, meditation, and regular exercise can help lower cortisol levels and promote a more fertile hormonal environment.

Even age plays a role in male fertility, though men can technically father children well into their later years. As men age, sperm quality naturally declines. Sperm motility decreases, and DNA fragmentation becomes more common. This means that while men may continue to produce sperm, the likelihood of conception decreases, and the risk of miscarriage or genetic abnormalities increases. Age may not place as rigid a limit on male fertility as it does on female fertility, but it remains an important factor, particularly for couples trying to conceive later in life.

In the end, male fertility is a combination of both numbers and quality. High sperm counts don't guarantee success, just as low sperm counts don't mean failure. The health of each individual sperm—its ability to swim, its shape, and its genetic integrity—matters just as much as the quantity produced. By understanding these nuances and taking steps to support both sperm count and quality, men can improve their chances of fathering a child and contributing to a successful conception journey.

Shared Factors in Fertility: Lifestyle, Health, and Timing

Although there are clear differences in how fertility manifests in men and women, it's important to recognize that several factors influence both genders in similar ways. The choices we make in our daily lives, including what we eat, how we stay active, and how we manage stress, are vital for supporting fertility in both men and women. A diet rich in nutrients plays a vital role in supporting the health of both eggs and sperm. Additionally, engaging in regular exercise helps maintain hormonal balance and alleviates stress, which is a well-known factor that can disrupt reproductive health.

Stress can significantly affect fertility in various ways. Chronic stress affects both men and women by increasing cortisol levels, which can disrupt the production of essential reproductive hormones such as estrogen, progesterone, and testosterone. Elevated stress levels can impact women's ovulation and men's sperm production, creating challenges for conception. Managing stress through techniques like meditation, mindfulness, or regular physical activity can greatly enhance fertility outcomes.

Your body weight can have a significant impact on your fertility. Maintaining a healthy weight is crucial, as being underweight or overweight can significantly impact hormonal balance. This disruption can influence ovulation in women and testosterone levels in men. Keeping a healthy body weight by following a balanced diet and engaging in regular exercise is a highly effective approach to enhancing fertility.

Ultimately, timing plays a critical role in the fertility journey. The "fertile window" for women refers to the few days each month when the chances of conception are highest, and this timing is closely linked to the regularity of ovulation. Monitoring ovulation using techniques such as basal body temperature, observing cervical mucus, or utilizing ovulation predictor kits can assist couples in identifying their peak fertile days. For men, while timing may not revolve around a monthly cycle, it remains important. Regular ejaculation every two to three days plays a significant role in maintaining healthy and fresh sperm, ultimately optimizing fertility.

By recognizing these factors, individuals and couples can actively work towards improving their fertility and increasing their chances of conception.

Key Nutrients for Fertility: Nourishing the Body for Conception

Fertility serves as a mirror to our overall health, fundamentally relying on the body's ability to receive the right nutrients that are essential for every phase of reproduction. These nutrients serve a vital role beyond merely providing energy; they function as essential building blocks, hormonal regulators, and guardians of cellular health. Both men and women can greatly benefit from maintaining a healthy balance of essential vitamins, minerals, and other nutrients, as this can play a crucial role in enhancing fertility and boosting the likelihood of conception. In this subchapter, we will delve into the vital nutrients that significantly impact fertility and their contributions to reproductive health.

Folate: The Guardian of Genetic Health

Folate plays a key role in supporting fertility and is considered one of the most important nutrients in this area. It is essential for the synthesis and repair of DNA, highlighting its importance not just during conception, but also throughout the entire pregnancy journey. Folate intervenes in the initial phases of cell division, helping to ensure that both sperm and eggs are created with healthy genetic material. For women, folate fosters a supportive environment for egg development, helping to ensure that the egg's DNA remains intact and primed for fertilization. For men it helps enhance sperm quality, increasing sperm count, and lowering the chances of chromosomal abnormalities.

Folate plays a critical role not only in DNA synthesis but also in safeguarding developing embryos from neural tube defects. Women are encouraged to boost their folate intake even before conception to ensure their bodies are well-prepared with this essential nutrient at the time of fertilization. Leafy green vegetables like spinach and kale, legumes such as lentils and chickpeas, and fortified grains are excellent sources of folate. If you're finding it challenging to meet your folate needs through diet alone, consider folic acid supplements as a helpful option for extra support.

Folate's role goes beyond just DNA synthesis. After fertilization takes place, folate plays an essential part in the initial stages of embryo development. It supports the rapid cell division that occurs during the initial days and weeks following conception. It's important for women to prioritize their folate intake even before they start trying to conceive. By the time pregnancy is confirmed, essential processes are already in motion, making early attention to nutrition vital. During this period, a lack of folate can heighten the risk of birth defects such as spina bifida. This is why healthcare professionals frequently advise women who are planning to conceive to take folic acid supplements. Folate from natural food sources, like dark leafy greens, beans, and fortified grains, is a wonderful way to enhance your nutrient reserves.

Folate stands out because of its significant effects on both men and women. Folate is essential for maintaining healthy sperm in men. Sperm cells, similar to eggs, experience swift cell division during their development, and folate ensures that this process happens accurately. It enhances sperm quality by decreasing DNA fragmentation, a condition where the DNA in sperm may be damaged or incomplete. This can potentially lead to fertility challenges or genetic concerns in future generations. Folate makes sure that every sperm cell is equipped with intact genetic material, which significantly enhances the likelihood of successful conception and promotes a healthy pregnancy. Folate is not merely a "women's vitamin"; it's a fertility enhancer for both partners on the journey to conception.

Zinc: The Fertility Powerhouse

Zinc is widely recognized for its significant influence on the reproductive systems of both men and women, earning it the title of fertility powerhouse. Zinc has a key role in reproductive health, yet it's a nutrient that often goes unnoticed in many people's diets. Understanding its importance can help you make more informed choices about your nutrition. The role it plays in fertility is complex, influencing various aspects such as hormone regulation and the health of both eggs and sperm.

Zinc is very important for men's health, particularly in supporting sperm production and the synthesis of testosterone. Testosterone serves as the main male sex hormone, playing a crucial role in sperm production, while zinc is an essential component in this important process. Insufficient zinc can result in a decline in testosterone levels, which may lead to a decrease in both sperm count and quality. Zinc not just increases sperm quantity, but also enhances sperm motility. This means it significantly impacts the sperm's ability to navigate effectively through the female reproductive system to reach the egg. Sperm that struggle to swim effectively face significant challenges in fertilizing an egg, regardless of their quantity. Zinc ensures that sperm are not only abundant but also active, which enhances the chances of successful fertilization.

Zinc not only enhances sperm count and motility but also serves a protective function. Sperm cells face significant challenges from oxidative stress, a situation in which free radicals—unstable molecules—can harm sperm DNA and cellular structures. This may reduce sperm viability and could potentially lead to genetic concerns in the offspring. Zinc serves as a powerful antioxidant, effectively neutralizing free radicals and safeguarding sperm from oxidative damage. The protective quality is vital for men facing environmental toxins or elevated stress levels, as both factors can intensify oxidative stress and negatively impact sperm quality.

Zinc is essential for female fertility as well, though its functions may vary slightly. Zinc plays a vital role in women's health by helping to regulate hormones and support the process of ovulation. Zinc assists in the hormonal processes that stimulate the release of eggs from the ovaries, helping to ensure that ovulation happens consistently and reliably. Lack of sufficient zinc can lead to irregularities in a woman's menstrual cycle, which may complicate the process of tracking ovulation and timing intercourse for conception. Zinc supports the development of healthy eggs, making sure they are strong and ready for fertilization.

Additionally, zinc plays a vital role in maintaining the health of the uterine lining, which is essential for the implantation and growth of a fertilized egg. Following ovulation, the uterine lining becomes thicker, readying itself for the potential arrival of an embryo. Zinc supports the structural integrity of this lining. When the uterine lining isn't sufficiently developed, it can lead to challenges with implantation, even in cases where fertilization has taken place. This emphasizes that fertility goes beyond simply achieving pregnancy; it involves fostering a nurturing environment where pregnancy can flourish—and zinc is fundamental in that process.

It's truly remarkable how easily we can incorporate zinc into our diets. You can find zinc in foods such as oysters, pumpkin seeds, beef, and legumes. These ingredients can be effortlessly integrated into your daily meals, allowing you to create a fertility-friendly diet that benefits both partners.

Omega-3 Fatty Acids: The Inflammation Fighters

Omega-3 fatty acids are widely recognized for their heart health benefits, yet their impact on fertility is just as significant. These vital fats act as the body's internal peacekeepers, working to combat inflammation and foster a balanced, harmonious environment that enhances the likelihood of conception. Chronic inflammation can significantly impact fertility for both men and women, acting as a major disruptor in the process. Inflammation can arise from various sources, such as stress, environmental toxins, or an inadequate diet, and it can significantly impact the reproductive system. This interference can influence aspects like the health of eggs and sperm, as well as the balance of hormones.

Chronic inflammation can significantly disrupt the intricate processes of ovulation and implantation in women. The reproductive system is highly delicate, and when inflammation increases, it can interfere with the hormonal signals that are essential for the release of eggs from the ovaries. Even when all other systems are working well, inflammation can still hinder or completely stop the process of ovulation. Additionally, inflammation can adversely affect the uterine lining, reducing its ability to accept a fertilized egg. In such situations, even when conception happens, the process of implantation might not occur, leading to a lost chance for pregnancy.

Omega-3 fatty acids play a vital role in reducing inflammation and helping to bring balance back to the body. Healthy fats, which are abundant in fatty fish such as salmon, mackerel, and sardines, along with plant-based sources like flaxseeds and walnuts, possess powerful anti-inflammatory benefits. These treatments function by managing the production of inflammatory molecules within the body, effectively soothing an overly active immune response. By reducing inflammation, we foster a more supportive environment for conception, enabling ovulation and implantation to occur more seamlessly.

Inflammation can significantly impact men's fertility, especially regarding the health of sperm. Sperm cells face significant challenges due to oxidative stress, commonly stemming from chronic inflammation. Oxidative stress has the potential to harm sperm DNA, decrease motility, and hinder the sperm's capacity to fertilize an egg. Omega-3 fatty acids safeguard sperm by offering anti-inflammatory and antioxidant benefits that help shield them from potential damage. The structural integrity of sperm cell membranes is critical, as it not only enables effective swimming but also provides essential protection against environmental and internal stressors that could compromise their viability.

In addition to their anti-inflammatory properties, omega-3 fatty acids are essential for hormone regulation, especially for women. Healthy fats assist in the production of prostaglandins, which are hormone-like compounds that help regulate various bodily functions, including the menstrual cycle. Omega-3s play a crucial role in regulating the production of the right types of prostaglandins in balanced amounts, which can lead to more predictable and reliable ovulation. For women on the journey to conceive, maintaining a regular ovulation cycle is important, as it significantly enhances the likelihood of successful conception.

Adding omega-3-rich foods to your daily diet can be a straightforward and impactful approach to enhancing fertility. When you choose to add salmon to your dinner plate, sprinkle flaxseeds into your morning smoothie, or enjoy walnuts as a snack, you're giving your body essential support to combat inflammation, balance hormones, and safeguard reproductive cells. Omega-3s serve as wonderful allies for fertility, fostering a serene and balanced environment that supports the journey toward conception.

Vitamin D: The Hormonal Regulator

Vitamin D is more than just a vitamin, it functions similarly to a hormone, impacting a wide range of areas including immune function, mood, and reproductive health. The capacity to regulate hormones makes it a vital nutrient for anyone aiming to improve their fertility.

Vitamin D plays a huge role for women in supporting hormonal balance, especially concerning estrogen and progesterone. These two essential hormones are key in regulating the menstrual cycle and preparing the body for pregnancy. When vitamin D levels are at their best, these hormones can work effectively, promoting regular ovulation and creating a welcoming uterine environment for implantation. When vitamin D levels are low, it can disrupt regular cycles, making it challenging to anticipate ovulation and potentially lowering the likelihood of conception. Studies indicate that women who maintain higher levels of vitamin D often experience improved fertility outcomes, whether through natural conception or assisted reproductive methods such as IVF.

However, the advantages of vitamin D go far beyond merely regulating the menstrual cycle. This nutrient has a vital role in supporting ovarian health, which is essential for maintaining egg quality. As women grow older, it's natural for the quality of their eggs to decline. However, ensuring sufficient levels of vitamin D can help slow this process, potentially enhancing the chances of successful conception in the future. Vitamin D plays a crucial role in ensuring that the eggs released during ovulation are healthy and ready for fertilization. Vitamin D seems to serve as a protective shield for the ovaries, supporting their optimal function even as the body ages.

Vitamin D has a key role for men, especially regarding the production of testosterone. Research indicates that men who maintain adequate vitamin D levels often experience elevated testosterone levels, leading to enhancements in sperm production, motility, and overall fertility. Moreover, vitamin D helps improve sperm morphology, which refers to the shape and structure of sperm. This enhancement can lead to a higher likelihood of normal sperm, ultimately boosting the chances of successful fertilization.

Vitamin D supports fertility, particularly due to its connection with calcium. Calcium helps in various reproductive processes, such as egg maturation and sperm function, while vitamin D is vital for the body to effectively absorb and utilize calcium. Insufficient vitamin D can lead to imbalances in calcium levels, which may have an impact on reproductive health. Ensuring that you get enough vitamin D—whether through sunlight, your diet, or supplements—plays a crucial role in helping your body maintain the right calcium balance, which is essential for optimal fertility.

Vitamin D deficiency is more common than many realize, particularly in areas with less sunlight, and it can significantly affect fertility. For those residing in regions with extended winters or who find themselves indoors for much of the time, obtaining sufficient vitamin D from sunlight alone can be quite challenging. In these situations, including vitamin D-rich foods such as fatty fish, fortified dairy products, and egg yolks can be beneficial. However, it might also be important to consider supplementation to achieve optimal levels.

Antioxidants: Protecting Reproductive Cells

Antioxidants serve as essential allies in the realm of fertility, safeguarding the intricate elements of our reproductive health with their protective qualities. To grasp their significance, consider antioxidants as the body's defense system—vital agents actively engaged in the fight against cellular damage. Each day, our bodies encounter free radicals—unstable molecules that can lead to oxidative stress. Free radicals can come from a variety of sources, such as environmental toxins, pollution, stress, and even the foods we consume. In limited quantities, free radicals pose no threat, but when their levels escalate beyond control, they can cause significant damage to cells, including those vital for reproduction.

Reproductive cells, such as eggs and sperm, are especially susceptible to oxidative stress in both men and women. Here is where antioxidants come into play. Antioxidants play a crucial role in our health by neutralizing free radicals, disarming these potentially harmful agents before they can inflict damage. Oxidative stress can significantly impact women's reproductive health by damaging eggs, which may result in lower egg quality or even chromosomal abnormalities. As we age, our bodies experience a natural increase in oxidative stress, which contributes to the decline in egg quality over time. By incorporating foods that are high in antioxidants into their diets, women can help protect their eggs, slowing down damage and preserving their reproductive potential for a longer time.

For men, the stakes are equally significant. Sperm cells, much like eggs, are particularly vulnerable to oxidative stress. When free radicals strike, it can lead to damaged DNA or hindered motility, which is a significant concern for reproductive health. Sperm that have fragmented or damaged DNA face significant challenges in successfully fertilizing an egg. Even when fertilization does take place, there is a heightened risk of miscarriage or genetic abnormalities. Antioxidants play a critical role in protecting against damage, helping to keep sperm healthy, agile, and ready for fertilization. Research indicates that men who include a diet abundant in antioxidants often experience enhanced sperm quality, improved motility, and increased sperm counts, all of which can significantly elevate the chances of conception.

Antioxidants are truly a gift from nature, and adding them to your diet can be an enjoyable and straightforward experience. Berries are a wonderful choice, as they are rich in powerful antioxidants like vitamin C and flavonoids. These nutrients play a crucial role in safeguarding reproductive cells from oxidative damage. Blueberries, strawberries, and raspberries stand out as powerful choices, effortlessly enhancing any diet aimed at supporting fertility. Dark leafy greens like spinach and kale are packed with vitamins E and C—two essential antioxidants that support fertility for both men and women by helping to reduce oxidative stress in reproductive tissues.

Nuts and seeds offer a fantastic source of antioxidants, particularly when it comes to vitamin E. This fat-soluble vitamin safeguards the cell membranes of both eggs and sperm, offering an important layer of protection against oxidative damage. For men, vitamin E enhances sperm function, leading to improved motility and morphology. In women, it is essential for maintaining ovarian tissue health and supporting a regular menstrual cycle. Adding almonds, sunflower seeds, or walnuts to your daily meals can be an easy yet effective method to enhance your antioxidant intake.

Antioxidants like selenium, which can be found in Brazil nuts and seafood, as well as beta-carotene, present in carrots and sweet potatoes, play a vital role in enhancing fertility. They support immune function and promote overall cellular health, making them important for those looking to improve their reproductive well-being. Selenium serves a vital dual purpose in fertility, functioning as an antioxidant while also being essential for sperm production. This process plays a crucial role in safeguarding the testes from oxidative damage, creating a healthier environment for sperm production and reducing their vulnerability to harm.

Iron: The Blood Builder

Iron is frequently referred to as the "blood builder," and there's a solid rationale behind this designation. This mineral plays a key role in one of the body's most important functions: the creation of hemoglobin, the protein found in red blood cells that transports oxygen throughout the body, reaching even the reproductive organs. Lack of sufficient iron can hinder the body's ability to produce adequate hemoglobin, which may result in feelings of fatigue, weakness, and, importantly, a decrease in fertility. For women, it's important to keep iron levels in check, especially since menstruation can naturally reduce iron stores every month. When these stores aren't replenished through diet or supplements, women may face the risk of developing iron deficiency, potentially leading to a condition called anemia.

Anemia goes beyond the constant fatigue many experience; it can significantly affect a woman's chances of conception. When the body experiences low iron levels, it focuses on crucial functions, such as supplying oxygen to the brain and heart, rather than on reproductive processes. This may lead to irregular or even absent ovulation, as the body recognizes that it's not in the best condition for pregnancy. When regular ovulation is absent, the likelihood of conceiving decreases significantly. Additionally, if conception does happen, low iron levels may heighten the risk of complications, such as early pregnancy loss. When you make sure your body has sufficient iron, you're not just boosting your energy and overall well-being; you're also providing your reproductive system with the oxygen-rich blood flow essential for its proper function.

The significance of iron continues well beyond the moment of conception. Throughout pregnancy, a woman's blood volume expands by almost 50% to nurture the developing fetus, which significantly raises the need for iron. Women starting their pregnancy with low iron levels face an increased risk of severe anemia, which can result in preterm birth, low birth weight, and various other complications. Building up iron stores before conception is essential. It lays the groundwork for a healthy pregnancy, ensuring that both the mother and baby receive the oxygen necessary for their well-being.

Iron plays a significant role for men as well, even if its impact on fertility isn't as straightforward. Iron deficiency may be less frequent in men, but it is still a possibility, particularly for those who have inadequate diets or existing health issues. Iron supports the reproductive system by ensuring that tissues receive the oxygen they need to function effectively. Although iron may not be directly associated with sperm production like some other nutrients, keeping your iron levels healthy is important for overall body function. This, in turn, fosters a more supportive environment for sperm production.

It's encouraging to know that iron can be found in a variety of foods, which makes it quite simple to add to your diet. For meat eaters, red meat, especially beef and lamb, stands out as one of the richest sources of heme iron, which is the form of iron that the body absorbs most efficiently. If you're a vegetarian or someone who enjoys plant-based options, you'll be pleased to know that iron is abundant in legumes like lentils and chickpeas, along with dark leafy greens such as spinach. Non-heme iron, which is present in plant-based foods, is not absorbed by the body as easily. Therefore, it's beneficial to combine these foods with options rich in vitamin C to enhance absorption. For instance, incorporating a squeeze of lemon juice into your spinach salad or combining lentils with bell peppers can greatly improve your body's capacity to absorb iron.

If you're finding it challenging to meet your iron needs through diet alone, consider that iron supplements might offer a supportive option for you. It's essential to talk to a healthcare provider before beginning any supplements, as excessive iron intake can result in toxicity and various health complications. Finding the right balance in iron intake is essential. While insufficient iron can impact fertility, excessive amounts can lead to complications too.

Magnesium: The Stress Reliever

Magnesium is commonly known as nature's chill pill, and there's a solid reason behind this reputation. This mineral is essential for overall well-being, and its impact on fertility is particularly significant. In today's fast-paced world, where stress and anxiety have become all too familiar, the importance of magnesium as a natural stress reliever cannot be overstated. Magnesium plays a crucial role in fertility due to its capacity to aid the body's stress response and maintain hormonal balance—both of which are vital for optimal reproductive health.

Stress highly affects fertility, yet it is frequently underestimated. Stress can arise from various aspects of our lives, including work, personal challenges, or the emotional journey of trying to conceive. During these times, our bodies respond by releasing cortisol. Elevated cortisol levels can disrupt the intricate harmony of reproductive hormones. In women, higher cortisol levels can disrupt the communication between the brain and the ovaries, potentially delaying or even preventing ovulation. In certain situations, this can make conception extremely challenging. Cortisol can have a significant effect on men by reducing testosterone levels, which in turn directly influences both sperm production and quality.

Magnesium plays a vital role as a natural ally in managing stress. Magnesium regulates cortisol production, guiding the body to relax and restore its natural balance. When cortisol levels are effectively managed, the body's reproductive hormones can operate as they are meant to. For women, this translates to more consistent ovulation, while for men, it leads to healthier testosterone levels and enhanced sperm production. Ensuring that your body receives adequate magnesium can play a significant role in reducing the adverse effects of stress on fertility. This allows your body to prioritize reproduction over survival, creating a more supportive environment for conception.

Magnesium offers a range of benefits beyond just alleviating stress. This mineral is essential for muscle function, offering valuable support for women who may be dealing with painful menstrual cramps or other discomforts associated with their reproductive cycle. Magnesium plays a vital role in relaxing smooth muscle tissue, including the muscles of the uterus. This can help alleviate cramping and contribute to a more comfortable menstrual cycle. This is particularly beneficial for women experiencing conditions such as endometriosis or polycystic ovary syndrome (PCOS), where muscle tension and discomfort are frequent.

Beyond its soothing properties, magnesium promotes overall hormonal health. It helps regulate insulin, a hormone essential for keeping blood sugar levels in check. Unstable blood sugar levels can contribute to insulin resistance, which is often associated with PCOS and various fertility challenges. Magnesium plays a crucial role in stabilizing insulin levels, fostering a more balanced hormonal environment that can enhance reproductive outcomes for both men and women.

Magnesium can be found in a variety of nutrient-rich foods, which makes it quite simple to include in your daily meals. Dark leafy greens such as spinach, kale, and Swiss chard provide a fantastic source of magnesium. Nuts and seeds, especially almonds, pumpkin seeds, and flaxseeds, are excellent sources of this essential mineral. If you're seeking a delicious way to boost your magnesium intake, dark chocolate is an excellent choice, providing not only delightful flavor but also potential fertility benefits. Incorporating magnesium-rich foods into your diet can be key in alleviating stress, regulating hormones, and ultimately improving fertility.

Selenium: Supporting Sperm and Egg Health

Selenium may not be the most commonly discussed nutrient, yet its importance in fertility is undeniable. It significantly contributes to the health and vitality of both sperm and eggs, making it an important factor in reproductive health. This trace mineral serves as a potent antioxidant, playing a crucial role in safeguarding cells, especially reproductive cells, from oxidative damage. Selenium protects these cells from damage, helping to keep them healthy and functional, which is essential for achieving conception.

Selenium supports optimal sperm health in men. Selenium plays a vital role in selenoproteins, which are essential for safeguarding sperm against oxidative damage and maintaining their structural integrity. For sperm cells to be healthy and effectively swim toward the egg, they rely on strong, well-functioning mitochondria, which serve as the energy powerhouse of the cell. Selenium is directly involved in supporting this essential process. Lack of sufficient selenium can significantly hinder sperm motility, which is crucial for their ability to swim effectively. This reduction can greatly diminish the likelihood of sperm successfully reaching and fertilizing the egg.

Selenium impacts sperm morphology, influencing the shape and structure of sperm. Having the right morphology is critical for sperm to successfully penetrate the egg during fertilization. When sperm are misshapen or have structural abnormalities, their likelihood of achieving successful fertilization decreases considerably.

Selenium plays a crucial role for women, especially regarding the health of their eggs. Selenium safeguards eggs from oxidative stress, helping to keep the egg's DNA intact and undamaged, much like it does for sperm. As women grow older, it's important to understand that the quality of their eggs naturally diminishes, and this decline can be hastened by oxidative stress. Incorporating selenium into a fertility-focused diet can be a valuable step for women looking to slow down the decline in egg health, ultimately enhancing the chances of successful fertilization.

In addition to its benefits for egg health, selenium is also vital for the thyroid gland, which is essential in managing reproductive hormones. The thyroid plays a vital role in producing hormones that affect metabolism, energy levels, and, importantly, fertility. An underactive or overactive thyroid can cause hormonal imbalances that interfere with ovulation and menstrual cycles, which can pose challenges when trying to conceive. Selenium aids in the conversion of the hormone thyroxine (T4) into its active form, triiodothyronine (T3). Maintaining this balance is essential for the thyroid to function effectively, ultimately contributing to overall reproductive health.

Incorporating foods rich in selenium into your daily routine can be quite simple and rewarding. Brazil nuts stand out as a remarkable source of selenium—consuming just one or two nuts daily can deliver your complete requirement of this vital mineral. In addition to those, you can find selenium in sunflower seeds, tuna, eggs, and whole grains such as brown rice and oats. Incorporating these foods into your diet consistently helps ensure that your reproductive cells receive the essential support they require to remain healthy and operate optimally.

Nourishing our bodies with the right nutrients each day plays a vital role in the journey to conception. Understanding the importance of specific vitamins, minerals, and other nutrients in fertility can empower couples to make thoughtful dietary choices that may improve their chances of conceiving. Every nutrient matters for reproductive health, whether by helping to maintain hormonal balance, enhancing the quality of eggs and sperm, or minimizing the effects of oxidative stress. Focusing on a nutrient-rich diet allows couples to establish a solid foundation for fertility, fostering an environment where conception becomes not just possible, but highly likely. By embracing intentional eating, we can truly nourish our bodies and provide ourselves with the best opportunity to thrive on the journey to parenthood.

Dietary Do's and Don'ts: A Guide for Enhancing Fertility

Your diet plays a crucial role in enhancing fertility, often holding equal weight to medical interventions and lifestyle adjustments. Food is extremely important for our overall health and for individuals aiming to conceive, adopting a fertility-focused diet can foster an internal environment that enhances the chances of conception. The decisions we make while shopping for groceries and preparing meals significantly influence our hormonal balance, the quality of our eggs and sperm, and the overall health of our reproductive system. In this section, we will explore the essential dietary "do's and don'ts" for those on the journey to parenthood, providing clear and supportive guidance on what to embrace and what to steer clear of.

The Do's: Fertility-Enhancing Foods to Embrace

Embracing a nutrient-rich, whole-foods diet can be one of the most impactful changes you make on your fertility journey. It's important to select foods that are minimally processed and rich in vitamins, minerals, and antioxidants, as these can greatly support reproductive health. Begin by focusing on vibrant, fresh fruits and vegetables. The bright colors of fruits and vegetables do more than please the eye—they signal a wealth of antioxidants such as vitamin C, beta-carotene, and flavonoids, which are beneficial for our health. Antioxidants play a crucial role in safeguarding eggs and sperm from oxidative stress, enhancing their quality and viability. Dark leafy greens such as spinach, kale, and Swiss chard offer remarkable benefits, packed with folate, magnesium, and a variety of nutrients that can enhance fertility.

Incorporating whole grains into your diet can be a wonderful addition for supporting fertility. Whole grains, such as quinoa, brown rice, oats, and whole wheat, are packed with nutrients that refined grains lack. They retain their fiber, B vitamins, and essential minerals like zinc and iron, making them a wholesome choice for your diet. These nutrients help maintain stable blood sugar levels, an essential factor for achieving hormonal balance. Processed foods can cause blood sugar spikes, which may contribute to insulin resistance. This condition is often associated with infertility issues, including polycystic ovary syndrome (PCOS). Opting for whole grains allows your body to achieve a consistent release of insulin, fostering a healthier hormonal balance.

Incorporating healthy fats is essential for a diet that supports fertility. Fats often face criticism, yet it's important to recognize that healthy fats play a crucial role in hormone production and maintaining balance in our bodies. Incorporating foods that are high in omega-3 fatty acids, like salmon, sardines, chia seeds, and walnuts, can significantly help in reducing inflammation and enhancing reproductive health. Omega-3s help regulate the production of hormones such as estrogen and progesterone, making them an essential part of your fertility diet. Avocados, olive oil, and nuts are excellent sources of monounsaturated fats, which have been associated with enhanced egg quality and improved sperm health. Incorporating these fats into your meals can support hormone stability and enhance your chances of conception.

Protein plays a significant role in supporting fertility. It's important to recognize that not all proteins are the same. Incorporating lean, plant-based proteins such as lentils, beans, chickpeas, can be a wonderful way to support reproductive health. Animal proteins can certainly contribute to a healthy diet, but selecting high-quality, organic sources is essential whenever you can. Choosing grass-fed beef, pasture-raised chicken, and wild-caught fish is a great option, as these choices are free from the added hormones and antibiotics often present in conventionally raised meats. The hormones found in non-organic meat can interfere with your body's natural hormonal balance. Choosing clean, high-quality protein sources can truly make a positive impact on your health.

Alongside prioritizing these nutrient-rich foods, it's important to ensure you're staying properly hydrated. Water supports every function of the body, including those related to reproduction. Staying properly hydrated is essential for maintaining healthy cervical mucus, which is key for effective sperm transport and fertility. Make it a goal to stay well-hydrated by drinking plenty of water during the day. You might also want to think about incorporating hydrating foods such as cucumbers, oranges, and watermelon into your meals for added benefits.

The Don'ts: Foods and Habits to Avoid

While the "don'ts" of a fertility-focused diet might appear overwhelming initially, grasping the reasons behind how specific foods and habits can affect your chances of conception can truly empower you. Instead of viewing these as limitations, try to see them as thoughtful decisions that remove barriers, creating a clearer and more straightforward journey toward pregnancy. The foods and habits you avoid can have a significant impact, just like the nutrient-rich choices you choose to embrace. Let's explore some of the common dietary pitfalls that can impact fertility and understand why steering clear of them is so important.

High levels of sugar and refined carbohydrates can significantly impact fertility, often leading to challenges in this important aspect of health. While treats like candy, pastries, soda, and white bread can provide a quick surge of energy, it's important to be aware of their hidden drawbacks: they can lead to swift increases in blood sugar and insulin levels. When blood sugar levels spike rapidly, the body reacts by releasing a significant amount of insulin to bring those levels back down. The ongoing fluctuations can contribute to insulin resistance, a situation in which your cells struggle to respond properly to insulin. Insulin resistance in men can significantly impact testosterone levels, which in turn may influence sperm production and quality. Reducing your intake of sugary snacks and refined carbs can play a significant role in stabilizing your blood sugar and insulin levels. This adjustment fosters a more balanced hormonal environment, which is essential for supporting fertility.

Trans fats can be a significant obstacle when trying to conceive. Trans fats, commonly found in a variety of processed foods, baked goods, and fried snacks, are well-known for their harmful impact on heart health. However, it's important to recognize that they can also pose significant risks to reproductive health. Unhealthy fats can lead to increased inflammation in the body, which may disrupt ovulation in women and negatively impact sperm quality in men. Trans fats can also play a role in insulin resistance, which may further complicate the hormonal imbalances that can affect your ability to conceive. Deciding to remove trans fats from your diet is an impactful choice that can help decrease inflammation and enhance your body's natural reproductive functions. Choose healthy fats such as those in avocados, nuts, and olive oil. These options offer essential nutrients for your body while minimizing inflammatory effects.

The discussion around alcohol and fertility can be quite complex, yet health experts generally agree on one important point: reducing or eliminating alcohol intake can greatly enhance your chances of conceiving. Alcohol disrupts the delicate balance of reproductive hormones, particularly estrogen and testosterone. For women, even moderate alcohol intake can disrupt the menstrual cycle and hinder ovulation, which can complicate the ability to identify fertile days. Alcohol consumption in men can lead to a reduction in testosterone levels, a decrease in sperm count, and a decline in sperm motility, all of which may negatively impact fertility. In addition to its hormonal impacts, alcohol significantly strains the liver. When the liver is occupied with processing alcohol, it can find it challenging to efficiently metabolize and eliminate excess hormones, which may result in additional imbalances. Reducing or completely avoiding alcohol can significantly enhance your body's ability to maintain hormonal balance, fostering a more nurturing environment for conception.

If you're on the journey to conceive, it might be worthwhile to take a closer look at your caffeine consumption. Although enjoying a daily cup of coffee or tea might appear to be innocuous, it's important to recognize that consuming too much caffeine can subtly yet significantly impact fertility. Caffeine acts as a stimulant, leading to an increase in stress hormones such as cortisol. This can disturb the delicate balance of reproductive hormones in the body. Elevated cortisol levels can disrupt ovulation, which may pose challenges for women trying to conceive. Research suggests that for men, consuming large amounts of caffeine may be associated with a decline in sperm quality. Moreover, caffeine can have a diuretic effect, which may result in dehydration. Maintaining proper hydration is essential for supporting healthy cervical mucus in women and ensuring optimal sperm function in men. If you're on your journey to conceive, it might be beneficial to lower your caffeine intake to just one cup a day. You could also explore herbal teas such as chamomile or peppermint, which provide a calming, caffeine-free option that can be quite comforting.

Avoiding processed foods is an important step to consider when you're focusing on enhancing fertility. Many of these foods are packed with a long list of artificial ingredients, such as preservatives, flavor enhancers, and chemical additives, which can interfere with endocrine function. Numerous processed foods contain elevated levels of added sugars, unhealthy fats, and refined carbohydrates. These components can contribute to insulin resistance and inflammation. Processed foods often lack fiber and essential nutrients, which means they provide minimal nourishment and can contribute to hormonal imbalances. Opting for whole, unprocessed foods allows your body to receive the essential nutrients it requires to nurture reproductive health and enhance the likelihood of a successful pregnancy.

The topic of soy products and their impact on fertility can be quite complex. Soy is rich in phytoestrogens, which are plant-based compounds that can imitate estrogen in the body. Moderate consumption of soy is typically safe, but it's important to be mindful that consuming large quantities of soy-based products—such as tofu, soy milk, and soy protein isolate—may result in an excess of estrogen-like compounds in the body. For women facing challenges such as estrogen dominance or PCOS, these conditions can intensify hormonal imbalances, which may create additional hurdles in the journey to conceive. Research suggests that for men, consuming a significant amount of soy products may be associated with lower testosterone levels and a decline in sperm quality. If you appreciate soy, it's wise to enjoy it in moderation and choose fermented options such as miso or tempeh. These choices are not only easier on digestion but also have a gentler effect on hormone levels.

It's important to recognize the impact of exposure to pesticides and environmental toxins found in our food. It's important to be aware that many conventionally grown fruits and vegetables are treated with pesticides, which have been associated with endocrine disruption. This can have implications for fertility in both men and women. These chemicals have the potential to imitate or disrupt natural hormones, which can result in imbalances that affect both ovulation and sperm production. To minimize your exposure to these toxins, consider choosing organic produce whenever you can, particularly for those items on the "Dirty Dozen" list, as they are more prone to pesticide contamination. Thoroughly washing your fruits and vegetables can significantly help in reducing pesticide residue. However, opting for organic produce is the most effective way to minimize your risk.

It's important to recognize that excessive salt intake is a frequently overlooked factor that can have a negative impact on fertility. Excessive sodium intake can result in water retention and dehydration, which can challenge the body's ability to stay properly hydrated. It's especially important for women to stay hydrated, as dehydration can affect the quality of cervical mucus. Dehydration can significantly impact men's health, particularly affecting semen quality by decreasing both the volume and motility of sperm. To manage your sodium intake effectively, it's best to steer clear of processed and packaged foods, as they often contain high levels of salt. Instead, consider enhancing your meals with herbs, spices, and natural flavorings for a healthier and more flavorful option.

Embracing these dietary changes might feel daunting initially, but the advantages you'll gain truly surpass any short-term discomfort. By cutting back on processed foods, trans fats, excessive sugar, alcohol, and caffeine, you are taking important steps to clear the path toward conception. It's not about denying yourself; it's about creating a supportive environment that lets your body's natural fertility flourish. These adjustments foster a cleaner, healthier internal environment that allows hormones to function at their best, supports the thriving of reproductive cells, and enables your body to concentrate on the incredible journey of creating life.

Crafting a fertility-friendly diet is all about embracing a balanced approach, allowing yourself to enjoy the foods you cherish while making mindful choices. It's all about choosing wisely in ways that truly nurture your body and enhance your reproductive health. Focusing on whole, nutrient-rich foods while avoiding inflammatory, processed, and sugary options creates a supportive foundation for a healthier hormonal balance. This approach can enhance egg and sperm quality, ultimately increasing the chances of conception.

Consistency plays a key role as well. Enjoying a treat or indulging in your favorite food every now and then won't jeopardize your chances of conceiving. However, it's important to consider the overall pattern of your diet. Every small choice we make each day contributes to shaping our environment for fertility, whether it fosters support or presents challenges. By emphasizing the addition of vibrant vegetables, lean proteins, and healthy fats to your diet, you naturally reduce the intake of foods that may impede your fertility. This approach not only supports your journey to conception but also makes it more nourishing and fulfilling.

The path to conception is uniquely individual, and it's important to recognize that there isn't a universal solution that fits everyone. Listening to your body is essential; it's important to nourish it with the best foods available and to be patient as you navigate this journey. By embracing a fertility-friendly diet, you're nurturing your body and creating an environment that supports new life, enhancing your chances for a healthy and joyful pregnancy.

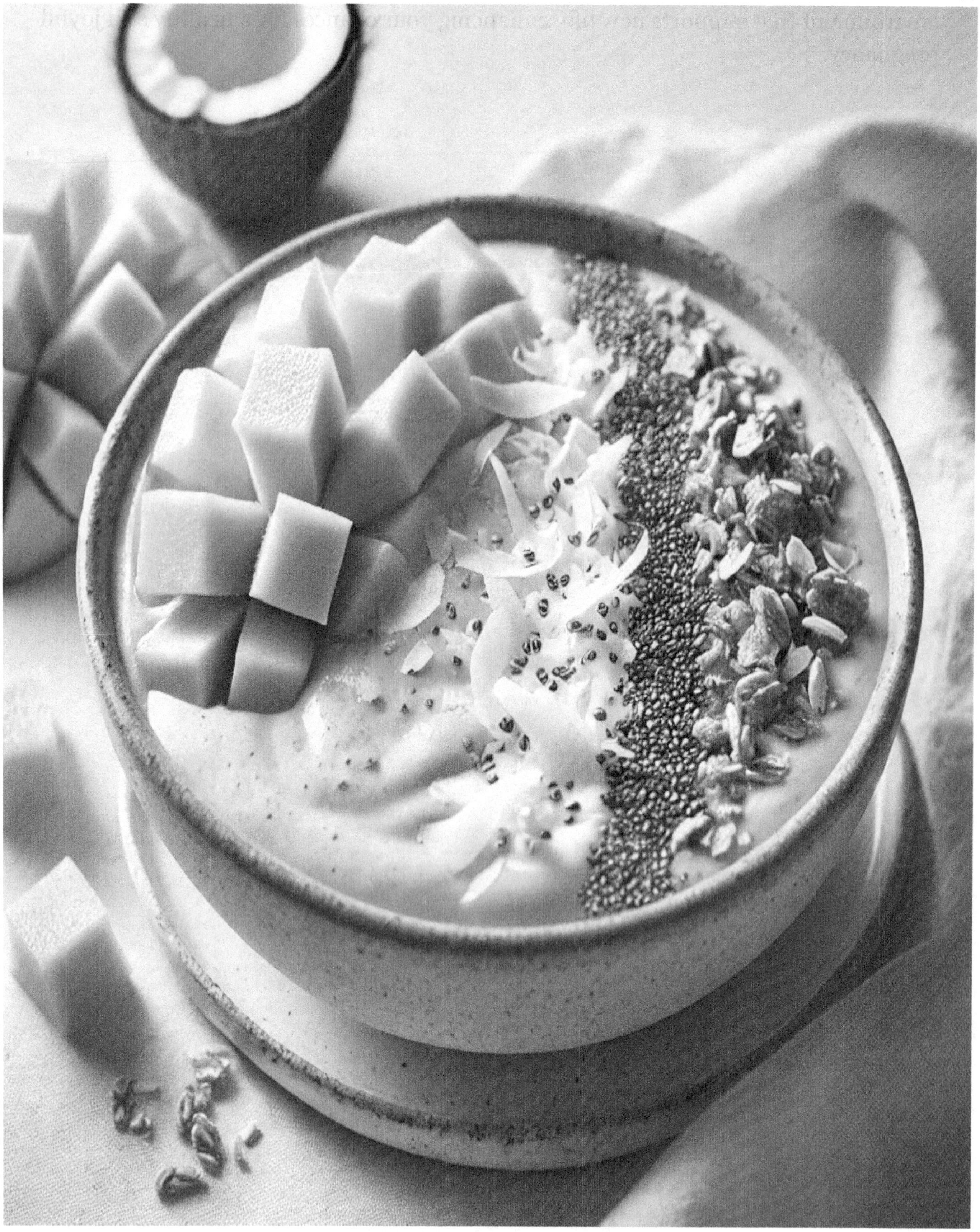

Chapter 3 Breakfasts to Kickstart Fertility

Breakfast sets the tone for how your body functions, metabolizes energy, and absorbs nutrients throughout the day. After a night of fasting, your body is primed to replenish energy stores and kick-start vital processes that influence everything from your blood sugar levels to hormonal balance. For those on a fertility journey, this morning ritual becomes even more critical. The right breakfast can stabilize blood sugar, balance hormone production, and deliver essential nutrients like folate, omega-3 fatty acids, magnesium, and protein—all of which play pivotal roles in reproductive health.

Eating a nutrient-dense breakfast not only provides immediate energy but also creates a foundation of stability for your body. Balanced blood sugar levels in the morning are essential for managing insulin sensitivity, which is intricately linked to hormonal health and ovulation. Starting your day with foods rich in antioxidants and anti-inflammatory properties can help combat oxidative stress, protecting reproductive cells and promoting an optimal environment for conception. Including healthy fats and complex carbohydrates can further fuel your body while providing a slow, sustained release of energy to keep you feeling satisfied and focused.

Moreover, breakfast offers an opportunity to pack in key fertility-boosting nutrients that are often harder to include in other meals.
The recipes in this section have been thoughtfully crafted to do more than just satisfy hunger. They are designed to nourish your body on a cellular level, optimize reproductive health, and keep your energy levels steady throughout the morning. Each recipe incorporates a variety of fertility-enhancing ingredients, from antioxidant-rich berries and leafy greens to protein-packed eggs and omega-3-laden seeds. Whether you're preparing a hearty breakfast bowl, a refreshing smoothie, or a simple nutrient-dense toast, these meals will help you start your day with intention and purpose.

Let's dive into a selection of breakfast recipes that are not only bursting with flavor but also carefully designed to provide the nutrients and energy your body needs to thrive. These recipes prove that fertility-friendly eating can be both enjoyable and transformative.

1. Fertility Power Smoothie

This smoothie is a fertility powerhouse. The combination of berries, spinach, and chia seeds offers antioxidants, omega-3 fatty acids, and folate, all of which protect reproductive cells and support hormonal balance. Almond butter and banana provide healthy fats and potassium for steady energy.

Prep Time: 5 minutes
Cooking Time: 0 minutes
Servings: 1

Ingredients:

- 1 cup unsweetened almond milk
- 1 cup mixed berries (blueberries, raspberries, strawberries)
- 1 handful fresh spinach
- 1 tablespoon chia seeds
- 1 banana
- 1 tablespoon almond butter
- 1 teaspoon maca powder (optional)
- Ice cubes

Instructions:

1. Place all ingredients in a blender.
2. Blend on high speed until smooth and creamy.
3. Taste and adjust sweetness with honey or maple syrup if needed.
4. Pour into a glass and enjoy immediately.

Nutritional Facts (per serving):

Calories: 320
Protein: 8g
Carbs: 46g
Fat: 14g

Key Nutrients:

Omega-3 fatty acids (chia seeds)
Folate (spinach, berries)
Potassium (banana)

Tips:
For an extra protein boost, add a scoop of plant-based protein powder. Substitute almond butter with sunflower seed butter for a nut-free option.

2. Avocado and Egg Breakfast Bowl

Avocado provides hormone-supporting monounsaturated fats, and eggs are a rich source of high-quality protein and choline, which are critical for egg quality and fetal brain development.

Prep Time: 10 minutes
Cooking Time: 10 minutes
Servings: 1

Ingredients:

- 1 ripe avocado
- 2 large eggs
- 1 cup baby spinach
- 1/2 cup cherry tomatoes, halved
- 1 tablespoon olive oil
- Salt and pepper, to taste
- Fresh lemon juice (optional)
- 1 slice whole-grain toast (optional)

Instructions:

1. Heat olive oil in a skillet over medium heat. Sauté spinach and cherry tomatoes until the spinach wilts and the tomatoes soften.
2. Cook eggs to your preference (fried, scrambled, or poached) in a separate pan.
3. Slice avocado and mash with salt, pepper, and a squeeze of lemon juice.
4. Assemble the bowl with the mashed avocado, sautéed vegetables, and cooked eggs. Serve with toast if desired.

Nutritional Facts (with toast):

Calories: 420
Protein: 16g
Carbs: 28g
Fat: 32g

Key Nutrients:

Monounsaturated fats (avocado)
Choline (eggs)
Fiber (spinach, whole-grain toast)

Tips:
Sprinkle red pepper flakes for a touch of heat, or add microgreens for an extra nutrient boost.

3. Fertility Boost Oatmeal

Rich in fiber, omega-3 fatty acids, and antioxidants, this oatmeal helps regulate blood sugar and supports hormonal balance. Walnuts and flaxseeds provide additional healthy fats for reproductive health.

Prep Time: 5 minutes
Cooking Time: 7 minutes
Servings: 1

Ingredients:

- 1/2 cup rolled oats
- 1 cup almond milk
- 1 tablespoon ground flaxseeds
- 1 tablespoon chia seeds
- 1/2 teaspoon cinnamon
- 1/2 banana, sliced
- 1/4 cup fresh berries
- 1 tablespoon chopped walnuts

Instructions:

1. Combine oats, almond milk, flaxseeds, chia seeds, and cinnamon in a small pot.
2. Bring to a simmer over medium heat, stirring frequently until creamy (5-7 minutes).
3. Pour into a bowl and top with banana slices, fresh berries, and walnuts.

Nutritional Facts:

Calories: 350
Protein: 9g
Carbs: 54g
Fat: 14g

Key Nutrients:

Fiber (oats, flaxseeds)
Omega-3 fatty acids (chia seeds, walnuts)
Antioxidants (berries)

Tips:
For added sweetness, drizzle with a teaspoon of honey or maple syrup. Swap almond milk for coconut milk for a creamier texture.

4. Chia Seed Pudding with Berries

This pudding is loaded with omega-3 fatty acids from chia seeds and antioxidants from berries, which reduce inflammation and protect reproductive cells.

Prep Time: 5 minutes
Cooking Time: 4 hours (chilling time)
Servings: 2

Ingredients:

- 1/4 cup chia seeds
- 1 cup unsweetened almond milk
- 1 tablespoon maple syrup (optional)
- 1/2 teaspoon vanilla extract
- 1/2 cup mixed berries
- 1 tablespoon raspberry puree (optional)
- Fresh mint leaves for garnish

Instructions:

1. Whisk chia seeds, almond milk, maple syrup, and vanilla extract in a bowl until evenly combined.
2. Cover and refrigerate for at least 4 hours or overnight.
3. Stir the pudding and layer into serving glasses with raspberry puree (if using) and berries.
4. Garnish with mint and serve chilled.

Nutritional Facts (per serving):

Calories: 250
Protein: 6g
Carbs: 30g
Fat: 12g

Key Nutrients:

Omega-3 fatty acids (chia seeds)
Antioxidants (berries)
Calcium (almond milk)

Tips:
Add granola for crunch or coconut flakes for an extra tropical twist. Use any seasonal berries for variety.

5. Sweet Potato and Black Bean Breakfast Hash

Sweet potatoes are a fantastic source of beta-carotene, promoting hormonal balance. Black beans provide plant-based protein and folate, essential for healthy cell division.

Prep Time: 10 minutes
Cooking Time: 20 minutes
Servings: 2

Ingredients:

- 1 medium sweet potato, diced
- 1/2 cup black beans
- 1/2 red bell pepper, diced
- 1/4 red onion, diced
- 2 tablespoons olive oil
- 1 teaspoon cumin
- Salt and pepper, to taste
- Fresh cilantro, for garnish

Instructions:

1. Heat olive oil in a skillet over medium heat. Add sweet potato and cook for 10 minutes, stirring often.
2. Add bell pepper and onion, cooking for another 5 minutes until tender.
3. Stir in black beans, cumin, salt, and pepper, and cook for an additional 2-3 minutes.
4. Serve hot, garnished with fresh cilantro.

Nutritional Facts (per serving):

Calories: 360
Protein: 9g
Carbs: 52g
Fat: 14g

Key Nutrients:

Beta-carotene (sweet potato)
Folate (black beans)
Vitamin C (red bell pepper)

Tips:
Add a poached egg on top for extra protein and flavor. Use sweet paprika for a smoky twist.

6. Protein-Packed Greek Yogurt Parfait

This parfait combines Greek yogurt's probiotics and protein with antioxidant-rich berries and omega-3-packed chia seeds. It's a nutrient-dense way to start your day.

Prep Time: 5 minutes
Cooking Time: 0 minutes
Servings: 1

Ingredients:

- 1 cup Greek yogurt
- 1/2 cup granola
- 1 tablespoon chia seeds
- 1/4 cup mixed berries
- 1 teaspoon honey

Instructions:

1. In a glass or bowl, layer Greek yogurt, granola, chia seeds, and mixed berries.
2. Drizzle honey over the top.
3. Serve immediately for a quick, protein-rich breakfast or snack.

Nutritional Facts:

Calories: 320
Protein: 20g
Carbs: 38g
Fat: 10g

Key Nutrients:

Protein (Greek yogurt)
Omega-3 fatty acids (chia seeds)
Antioxidants (berries)

Tips:
Swap granola with crushed nuts for a lower-carb option. Use unsweetened yogurt to reduce sugar content.

7. Spinach and Mozzarella Omelette

Eggs provide high-quality protein and choline for reproductive health, while spinach delivers folate, supporting healthy cell division. Mozzarella adds calcium for hormonal balance.

Prep Time: 5 minutes
Cooking Time: 5 minutes
Servings: 1

Ingredients:

- 2 large eggs
- 1/4 cup fresh spinach, chopped
- 1/4 cup shredded mozzarella cheese
- 1 tablespoon milk (optional, for fluffier eggs)
- 1 tablespoon olive oil or butter
- Salt and pepper, to taste

Instructions:

1. Whisk eggs, milk (if using), salt, and pepper until frothy.
2. Heat olive oil or butter in a non-stick skillet over medium heat. Sauté spinach until wilted (1-2 minutes).
3. Pour the eggs into the skillet, swirling to cover the bottom. Let cook until the edges set.
4. Sprinkle mozzarella over one side, fold the omelette, and cook for another 30 seconds.
5. Slide onto a plate and serve immediately.

Nutritional Facts:

Calories: 300
Protein: 18g
Carbs: 3g
Fat: 24g

Key Nutrients:

Choline (eggs)
Folate (spinach)
Calcium (mozzarella)

Tips:
Add sautéed mushrooms or diced tomatoes for extra nutrients and flavor.

8. Banana Almond Butter Toast

This toast balances healthy fats from almond butter, potassium from bananas, and omega-3s from chia seeds, supporting stable energy levels and hormonal health.

Prep Time: 5 minutes
Cooking Time: 2 minutes (toasting)
Servings: 1

Ingredients:

- 1 slice whole-grain bread
- 2 tablespoons almond butter
- 1 banana, sliced
- 1 teaspoon chia seeds

Instructions:

1. Toast the whole-grain bread until golden brown.
2. Spread almond butter evenly on the toast.
3. Arrange banana slices on top and sprinkle with chia seeds.
4. Serve immediately.

Nutritional Facts:

Calories: 340
Protein: 10g
Carbs: 42g
Fat: 18g

Key Nutrients:

Potassium (banana)
Healthy fats (almond butter)
Fiber (whole-grain bread)

Tips:
For extra flavor, sprinkle with a pinch of cinnamon or drizzle with honey.

9. Quinoa Breakfast Bowl with Berries

Quinoa is a complete protein that supports muscle health and energy levels, while berries and flaxseeds add antioxidants and omega-3s for reproductive wellness.

Prep Time: 5 minutes
Cooking Time: 5 minutes
Servings: 1

Ingredients:

- 1/2 cup cooked quinoa
- 1/2 cup unsweetened almond milk
- 1/4 cup blueberries
- 1 tablespoon ground flaxseeds
- 1 tablespoon sliced almonds
- 1 teaspoon honey

Instructions:

1. Heat the cooked quinoa and almond milk in a small pot over medium heat until warm.
2. Transfer to a bowl and top with blueberries, flaxseeds, and sliced almonds.
3. Drizzle with honey before serving.

Nutritional Facts:

Calories: 280
Protein: 8g
Carbs: 42g
Fat: 9g

Key Nutrients:

Complete protein (quinoa)
Omega-3 fatty acids (flaxseeds)
Antioxidants (blueberries)

Tips:
Prepare quinoa in advance to save time in the morning. Substitute blueberries with raspberries or strawberries for variety.

10. Mango Coconut Smoothie Bowl

This tropical bowl is rich in beta-carotene, vitamin C, and healthy fats, which enhance egg health and stabilize hormones.

Prep Time: 5 minutes
Cooking Time: 0 minutes
Servings: 1

Ingredients:

- 1 cup frozen mango chunks
- 1/2 cup unsweetened coconut milk
- 1 tablespoon chia seeds
- 1/4 cup granola
- 1 tablespoon shredded coconut

Instructions:

1. Blend mango chunks and coconut milk until smooth.
2. Pour into a bowl and top with chia seeds, granola, and shredded coconut.
3. Serve immediately.

Nutritional Facts:

Calories: 350
Protein: 6g
Carbs: 58g
Fat: 15g

Key Nutrients:

Beta-carotene (mango)
Omega-3 fatty acids (chia seeds)
Healthy fats (coconut milk)

Tips:
Add a handful of spinach to the blend for extra nutrients without altering the flavor.

11. Blueberry Almond Overnight Oats

Overnight oats offer slow-releasing energy and stabilize blood sugar levels. Combined with blueberries' antioxidants and almond butter's healthy fats, this recipe is a fertility-boosting powerhouse.

Prep Time: 5 minutes
Cooking Time: 0 minutes (overnight chilling)
Servings: 1

Ingredients:

- 1/2 cup rolled oats
- 1/2 cup unsweetened almond milk
- 1/4 cup Greek yogurt
- 1/4 cup blueberries
- 1 tablespoon almond butter
- 1 teaspoon honey

Instructions:

1. In a jar or bowl, mix rolled oats, almond milk, and Greek yogurt until combined.
2. Stir in blueberries and almond butter.
3. Cover and refrigerate overnight.
4. In the morning, drizzle with honey and enjoy cold or warmed.

Nutritional Facts:

Calories: 330
Protein: 12g
Carbs: 48g
Fat: 12g

Key Nutrients:

Protein (Greek yogurt)
Antioxidants (blueberries)
Omega-3 fatty acids (almond butter)

Tips:
For added texture, sprinkle chopped almonds or chia seeds on top before serving.

12. Sweet Potato Pancakes

Sweet potatoes are high in beta-carotene, supporting hormone balance and cell growth. Paired with almond flour and eggs, these pancakes provide protein and healthy fats for reproductive health.

Prep Time: 10 minutes
Cooking Time: 10 minutes
Servings: 2

Ingredients:

- 1 cup mashed sweet potato
- 2 large eggs
- 1/4 cup almond flour
- 1/2 teaspoon cinnamon
- 1/4 teaspoon vanilla extract
- Coconut oil (for cooking)

Instructions:

1. In a bowl, mix mashed sweet potato, eggs, almond flour, cinnamon, and vanilla extract until smooth.
2. Heat coconut oil in a skillet over medium heat.
3. Pour small portions of the batter onto the skillet to form pancakes.
4. Cook for 2-3 minutes on each side until golden brown.
5. Serve with fresh fruit or a drizzle of maple syrup.

Nutritional Facts:

Calories: 320
Protein: 10g
Carbs: 42g
Fat: 14g

Key Nutrients:

Beta-carotene (sweet potato)
Protein (eggs)
Healthy fats (almond flour)

Tips:
Double the batch and freeze extras for quick weekday breakfasts.

13. Cinnamon Apple Quinoa Porridge

Quinoa is a complete protein, supporting energy and muscle health, while apples and walnuts add antioxidants and omega-3s to nourish reproductive cells.

Prep Time: 5 minutes
Cooking Time: 10 minutes
Servings: 1

Ingredients:

- 1/2 cup cooked quinoa
- 1/2 apple, diced
- 1 cup unsweetened almond milk
- 1/2 teaspoon cinnamon
- 1 tablespoon chopped walnuts

Instructions:

1. In a small pot, combine cooked quinoa, diced apple, almond milk, and cinnamon.
2. Heat over medium heat and bring to a simmer. Cook for 5-7 minutes, stirring occasionally, until the apple is tender.
3. Transfer to a bowl and top with chopped walnuts.

Nutritional Facts:

Calories: 300
Protein: 8g
Carbs: 48g
Fat: 10g

Key Nutrients:

Complete protein (quinoa)
Fiber (apple)
Omega-3 fatty acids (walnuts)

Tips:
Add a drizzle of honey or a handful of raisins for added sweetness.

14. Pumpkin Spice Fertility Muffins

Pumpkin provides beta-carotene for hormonal balance, while walnuts and almond flour add healthy fats and antioxidants that support reproductive health.

Prep Time: 10 minutes
Cooking Time: 25 minutes
Servings: 12 muffins

Ingredients:

- 1 cup pumpkin puree
- 2 large eggs
- 1/2 cup almond flour
- 1/2 cup rolled oats
- 1/4 cup maple syrup
- 1/4 cup Greek yogurt
- 1 teaspoon baking powder
- 1 teaspoon cinnamon
- 1/2 teaspoon nutmeg
- 1/4 cup dark chocolate chips (optional)
- 1/4 cup chopped walnuts

Instructions:

1. Preheat the oven to 350°F (175°C) and line a muffin tin with paper liners.
2. In a large bowl, whisk together pumpkin puree, eggs, maple syrup, and Greek yogurt.
3. Add almond flour, rolled oats, baking powder, cinnamon, and nutmeg to the wet ingredients and mix until smooth.
4. Fold in chocolate chips and walnuts.
5. Divide the batter evenly among the muffin cups.
6. Bake for 20-25 minutes or until a toothpick inserted into the center comes out clean.
7. Let cool before serving.

Nutritional Facts (per muffin):

Calories: 160
Protein: 5g
Carbs: 18g
Fat: 8g

Key Nutrients:

Beta-carotene (pumpkin)

Fiber (oats)
Antioxidants (dark chocolate chips)

Tips:
Store in an airtight container for up to three days or freeze for longer shelf life.

15. Turmeric Golden Milk Smoothie

Turmeric and ginger are anti-inflammatory spices that reduce oxidative stress, while chia seeds and almond butter provide omega-3s and healthy fats for hormone health.

Prep Time: 5 minutes
Cooking Time: 0 minutes
Servings: 1

Ingredients:

- 1 cup unsweetened almond milk
- 1 frozen banana
- 1 teaspoon turmeric powder
- 1/2 teaspoon ground ginger
- 1 tablespoon chia seeds
- 1 tablespoon almond butter
- 1 teaspoon honey (optional)
- Pinch of black pepper (to enhance turmeric absorption)
- Ice cubes

Instructions:

1. Combine all ingredients in a blender and blend on high speed until smooth and creamy.
2. Pour into a glass and serve immediately.

Nutritional Facts:

Calories: 300
Protein: 7g
Carbs: 40g
Fat: 14g

Key Nutrients:

Anti-inflammatory compounds (turmeric, ginger)
Omega-3 fatty acids (chia seeds)
Healthy fats (almond butter)

Tips:
For a spicier kick, add a pinch of cayenne pepper.

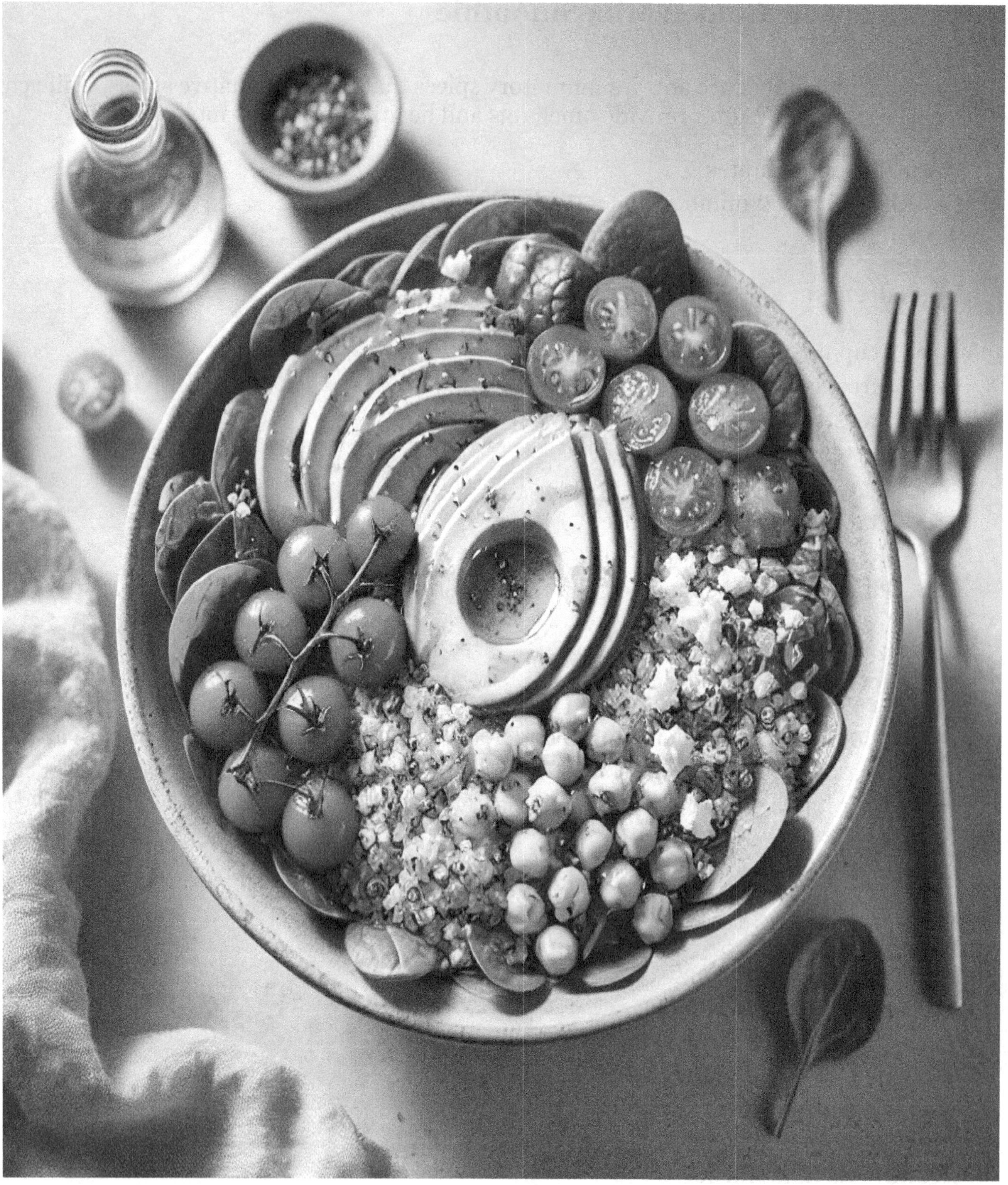

Chapter 4 Lunches Packed with Nutrients

Lunch is more than just a midday meal—it's an opportunity to reinforce your fertility journey with every bite. After the hustle of the morning, lunch serves as a critical moment to refuel your body, stabilize blood sugar levels, and deliver the essential nutrients that sustain energy and support hormonal health for the rest of the day. A well-balanced lunch is a powerful tool, ensuring your body remains nourished and resilient while supporting vital reproductive processes.

The recipes in this chapter are thoughtfully crafted to be nutrient-dense, satisfying, and easy to prepare, even on the busiest of days. They are packed with ingredients that not only nourish but also directly support fertility. From leafy greens loaded with folate and iron to lean proteins and fiber-rich legumes, these meals are designed to enhance egg and sperm quality, promote healthy hormonal balance, and create an ideal internal environment for conception.

These recipes go beyond basic sustenance; they are a celebration of vibrant, fertility-supporting foods. Whether you're enjoying a hearty salad, a comforting stew, or a creative wrap, each dish delivers an intentional blend of nutrients to support your body's reproductive health. For men, these lunches include ingredients like zinc-rich chickpeas and omega-3-rich salmon, which promote healthy testosterone levels and improve sperm quality. For women, folate-packed vegetables and hormone-balancing fats from avocado and olive oil are key players in fostering optimal egg health and hormonal equilibrium.

Moreover, lunch is a time to pause and reconnect with your goals. Preparing these recipes can be a moment of mindfulness, reinforcing the intention behind your fertility journey. Whether you're meal prepping for the week or crafting a fresh dish to savor in the moment, these lunches make the process of nourishing your body both practical and enjoyable. With these meals, you're not just feeding your body—you're empowering it, meal by meal, to create the best conditions for conception.

1. Quinoa and Chickpea Power Bowl

This bowl combines plant-based protein, folate, and fiber from quinoa and chickpeas, along with healthy fats from avocado, all of which help stabilize blood sugar and support hormone production.

Prep Time: 10 minutes
Cooking Time: 15 minutes
Servings: 2

Ingredients:

- 1 cup cooked quinoa
- 1/2 cup canned chickpeas, rinsed and drained
- 1 cup baby spinach
- 1/4 cup cherry tomatoes, halved
- 1/4 avocado, sliced
- 2 tablespoons crumbled feta cheese
- 1 tablespoon olive oil
- Juice of 1 lemon
- Salt and pepper to taste

Instructions:

1. Cook the quinoa according to package instructions and let it cool slightly.
2. In a large bowl, combine the quinoa, chickpeas, spinach, cherry tomatoes, avocado, and feta cheese.
3. In a small bowl, whisk together olive oil and lemon juice. Add salt and pepper to taste.
4. Drizzle the dressing over the quinoa mixture and toss gently to combine.
5. Serve immediately or refrigerate for up to 24 hours.

Nutritional Facts (per serving):

Calories: 420
Protein: 14g
Carbs: 50g
Fat: 18g

Key Nutrients:

Folate (chickpeas)
Fiber (quinoa, spinach)
Healthy fats (avocado, olive oil)

Tips:
For added crunch, sprinkle with roasted sunflower seeds or almonds.

---

2. Salmon and Avocado Salad

Salmon delivers omega-3 fatty acids that improve egg and sperm quality, while avocado provides monounsaturated fats that stabilize hormones.

Prep Time: 10 minutes
Cooking Time: 15 minutes
Servings: 2

Ingredients:

- 4 oz grilled or baked salmon
- 1/2 avocado, sliced
- 2 cups mixed greens (spinach, arugula, kale)
- 1/4 cup cherry tomatoes, halved
- 1/4 red onion, thinly sliced
- 1 tablespoon pumpkin seeds
- 2 tablespoons balsamic vinaigrette

Instructions:

1. Season and grill or bake the salmon until fully cooked (about 12-15 minutes). Let cool slightly.
2. In a large salad bowl, layer the greens, cherry tomatoes, red onion, and avocado slices.
3. Place the salmon on top and sprinkle with pumpkin seeds.
4. Drizzle with balsamic vinaigrette and toss gently before serving.

Nutritional Facts (per serving):

Calories: 450
Protein: 28g
Carbs: 14g
Fat: 32g

Key Nutrients:

Omega-3 fatty acids (salmon)
Zinc (pumpkin seeds)
Vitamin C (cherry tomatoes)

Tips:
For an extra flavor boost, add a squeeze of fresh lemon juice before serving.

---

3. Lentil and Sweet Potato Stew

This stew is packed with plant-based protein, iron from lentils, and beta-carotene from sweet potatoes, all essential for hormonal balance and healthy ovulation.

Prep Time: 15 minutes
Cooking Time: 30 minutes
Servings: 4

Ingredients:

- 1 cup red lentils
- 1 medium sweet potato, diced
- 1 carrot, diced
- 1 celery stalk, chopped
- 1/2 onion, diced
- 2 garlic cloves, minced
- 4 cups vegetable broth
- 1 teaspoon cumin
- 1 teaspoon turmeric
- Salt and pepper to taste
- Fresh cilantro for garnish

Instructions:

1. Heat a large pot over medium heat. Sauté the onion, garlic, carrot, and celery for 5 minutes until softened.
2. Add the diced sweet potato, lentils, cumin, and turmeric. Stir to coat.
3. Pour in the vegetable broth and bring to a boil. Reduce heat and simmer for 20-25 minutes, until the lentils and sweet potato are tender.
4. Season with salt and pepper, garnish with fresh cilantro, and serve hot.

Nutritional Facts (per serving):

Calories: 350
Protein: 15g
Carbs: 60g
Fat: 5g

Key Nutrients:

Iron (lentils)
Beta-carotene (sweet potato)
Anti-inflammatory compounds (turmeric)

Tips:
Pair with a slice of whole-grain bread for a heartier meal.

---

4. Mediterranean Chickpea Wrap

Rich in folate and plant-based protein, this wrap nourishes the reproductive system while offering a quick, satisfying meal.

Prep Time: 10 minutes
Cooking Time: None
Servings: 2

Ingredients:

- 1 whole-grain tortilla
- 1/2 cup canned chickpeas, rinsed and mashed
- 1/4 cup diced cucumber
- 1/4 cup diced tomatoes
- 2 tablespoons crumbled feta cheese
- 1 tablespoon hummus
- 1 tablespoon chopped parsley
- Salt and pepper to taste

Instructions:

1. Mash the chickpeas in a bowl and mix with diced cucumber, tomatoes, feta cheese, and parsley. Season with salt and pepper.
2. Spread hummus evenly over the tortilla.
3. Spoon the chickpea mixture onto the tortilla and roll tightly.
4. Slice in half and serve immediately.

Nutritional Facts (per serving):

Calories: 380
Protein: 14g
Carbs: 52g
Fat: 12g

Key Nutrients:

Folate (chickpeas)
Fiber (whole-grain tortilla)
Antioxidants (tomatoes)

Tips:
Add a handful of mixed greens for extra crunch and nutrients.

---

5. Avocado Tuna Salad

This protein-packed salad supports reproductive health with omega-3s from tuna, healthy fats from avocado, and probiotics from Greek yogurt.

Prep Time: 10 minutes
Cooking Time: None
Servings: 2

Ingredients:

- 1 can (5 oz) tuna in water, drained
- 1/2 avocado, mashed
- 1 celery stalk, finely chopped
- 1/4 red onion, diced
- 1 tablespoon Greek yogurt
- 1 teaspoon Dijon mustard
- Salt and pepper to taste
- Fresh lemon juice

Instructions:

1. In a medium bowl, combine tuna, mashed avocado, celery, and red onion.
2. Add Greek yogurt, Dijon mustard, salt, pepper, and a squeeze of fresh lemon juice. Mix well.
3. Serve on a bed of greens or with whole-grain crackers.

Nutritional Facts (per serving):

Calories: 320
Protein: 28g
Carbs: 8g
Fat: 20g

Key Nutrients:

Omega-3 fatty acids (tuna)
Fiber (avocado)
Probiotics (Greek yogurt)

Tips:
For a lighter option, use lettuce leaves as wraps instead of crackers.

---

6. Spinach and Quinoa Stuffed Peppers

This recipe is a nutrient powerhouse, combining quinoa and spinach for a perfect balance of plant-based protein, folate, and antioxidants to support egg and sperm health.

Prep Time: 10 minutes
Cooking Time: 25 minutes
Servings: 4

Ingredients:

- 2 bell peppers, halved and seeds removed
- 1 cup cooked quinoa
- 1 cup fresh spinach, chopped
- 1/2 cup diced tomatoes
- 1/4 cup black beans
- 1/4 cup shredded mozzarella cheese
- 1 tablespoon olive oil
- Salt and pepper to taste

Instructions:

1. Preheat the oven to 375°F (190°C).
2. In a medium bowl, mix together cooked quinoa, chopped spinach, diced tomatoes, black beans, olive oil, salt, and pepper.
3. Place the halved bell peppers on a baking sheet and stuff them with the quinoa mixture.
4. Sprinkle shredded mozzarella on top of each stuffed pepper.
5. Bake for 20-25 minutes, or until the peppers are tender and the cheese is melted.
6. Let cool slightly before serving.

Nutritional Facts (per serving):

Calories: 300
Protein: 12g
Carbs: 42g
Fat: 10g

Key Nutrients:

Folate (spinach)
Vitamin C (bell peppers)
Fiber (quinoa and black beans)

Tips:
Add a pinch of smoked paprika or chili flakes for extra flavor.

---

7. Fertility-Boosting Buddha Bowl

Packed with colorful vegetables and healthy fats, this bowl promotes hormonal balance and provides a variety of antioxidants to protect reproductive cells.

Prep Time: 15 minutes
Cooking Time: 20 minutes
Servings: 2

Ingredients:

- 1/2 cup cooked brown rice
- 1/2 cup roasted sweet potato cubes
- 1/4 cup steamed broccoli florets
- 1/4 cup sliced cucumber
- 1/4 avocado, sliced
- 1/4 cup edamame beans (shelled)
- 1 tablespoon tahini dressing
- 1 teaspoon sesame seeds
- Salt and pepper to taste

Instructions:

1. Roast the sweet potato cubes in the oven at 400°F (200°C) for 20 minutes, or until tender.
2. Steam the broccoli florets until bright green and slightly tender.
3. In a bowl, layer the cooked brown rice, roasted sweet potatoes, steamed broccoli, cucumber slices, avocado, and edamame.

4. Drizzle tahini dressing over the bowl and sprinkle with sesame seeds.
5. Season with salt and pepper, toss gently, and serve.

Nutritional Facts (per serving):

Calories: 420
Protein: 14g
Carbs: 60g
Fat: 16g

Key Nutrients:

Beta-carotene (sweet potatoes)
Phytoestrogens (edamame)
Antioxidants (broccoli)

Tips:
Substitute quinoa for brown rice if you prefer a grain-free option.

8. Lentil and Kale Soup

This soup provides a rich source of plant-based protein, iron, and folate from lentils and kale, making it ideal for supporting healthy ovulation and hormone regulation.

Prep Time: 10 minutes
Cooking Time: 40 minutes
Servings: 4

Ingredients:

- 1 cup green lentils
- 1 onion, diced
- 2 garlic cloves, minced
- 2 carrots, diced
- 2 celery stalks, chopped
- 1 can (14 oz) diced tomatoes
- 4 cups vegetable broth
- 2 cups chopped kale
- 1 teaspoon cumin
- 1/2 teaspoon smoked paprika
- Salt and pepper to taste
- 1 tablespoon olive oil

Instructions:

1. Heat olive oil in a large pot over medium heat. Add the onion, garlic, carrots, and celery, sautéing for about 5 minutes.
2. Stir in cumin and smoked paprika, and cook for another minute.
3. Add lentils, diced tomatoes, and vegetable broth. Bring to a boil, then reduce heat and simmer for 30 minutes.
4. Stir in chopped kale and simmer for another 5 minutes.
5. Season with salt and pepper, and serve hot.

Nutritional Facts (per serving):

Calories: 350
Protein: 18g
Carbs: 54g
Fat: 7g

Key Nutrients:

Iron (lentils)
Folate (kale)
Fiber (vegetables and lentils)

Tips:
Add a splash of lemon juice before serving to brighten the flavors.

---

9. Avocado Chicken Salad Wrap

This protein-packed wrap is filled with lean chicken, healthy fats from avocado, and probiotics from Greek yogurt to support hormonal health and gut balance.

Prep Time: 10 minutes
Cooking Time: None
Servings: 2

Ingredients:

- 1 cup cooked, shredded chicken breast
- 1/2 avocado, mashed
- 1/4 cup diced celery
- 1/4 cup diced apple
- 2 tablespoons Greek yogurt
- 1 teaspoon Dijon mustard
- Salt and pepper to taste
- 1 whole-grain tortilla
- Handful of mixed greens

Instructions:

1. In a bowl, combine shredded chicken, mashed avocado, celery, apple, Greek yogurt, and Dijon mustard.
2. Mix well and season with salt and pepper.
3. Lay the whole-grain tortilla flat, add the mixed greens, and spoon the chicken salad onto the tortilla.
4. Wrap tightly, slice in half, and serve.

Nutritional Facts (per serving):

Calories: 400
Protein: 28g
Carbs: 34g

Fat: 18g

Key Nutrients:

- Protein (chicken)
- Healthy fats (avocado)
- Fiber (whole-grain tortilla and celery)

Tips:
Replace the tortilla with a lettuce wrap for a low-carb option.

---

10. Fertility-Boosting Pesto Zoodles

This dish combines low-carb zucchini noodles with a basil pesto rich in healthy fats and antioxidants, which support cellular health and hormone production.

Prep Time: 10 minutes
Cooking Time: 5 minutes
Servings: 2

Ingredients:

- 2 medium zucchini, spiralized into noodles
- 1 cup fresh basil leaves
- 1/4 cup pine nuts
- 1/4 cup grated Parmesan cheese
- 1 garlic clove
- 1/4 cup olive oil
- Salt and pepper to taste
- 1/2 cup cherry tomatoes, halved

Instructions:

1. In a food processor, blend basil, pine nuts, Parmesan cheese, garlic, and olive oil until smooth. Season with salt and pepper.
2. Heat a skillet over medium heat and sauté the spiralized zucchini noodles for 2-3 minutes.
3. Toss the zoodles with the prepared pesto until evenly coated.
4. Add cherry tomatoes and cook for another minute.
5. Serve hot, garnished with extra Parmesan cheese if desired.

Nutritional Facts (per serving):

Calories: 350
Protein: 10g
Carbs: 14g
Fat: 30g

Key Nutrients:

Antioxidants (basil)
Healthy fats (pine nuts, olive oil)
Vitamin C (zucchini and cherry tomatoes)

Tips:
For added protein, top with grilled chicken or shrimp.

11. Black Bean and Avocado Quinoa Salad

This salad is a nutrient-packed combination of plant-based protein, fiber, and healthy fats, supporting hormonal balance and reducing inflammation.

Prep Time: 10 minutes
Cooking Time: None
Servings: 2

Ingredients:

- 1 cup cooked quinoa
- 1/2 cup black beans, rinsed and drained
- 1/2 avocado, diced
- 1/4 cup diced red bell pepper
- 1/4 cup diced red onion
- 1/4 cup fresh cilantro, chopped
- Juice of 1 lime
- 1 tablespoon olive oil
- Salt and pepper to taste

Instructions:

1. In a large bowl, combine the cooked quinoa, black beans, diced avocado, red bell pepper, red onion, and cilantro.
2. In a small bowl, whisk together lime juice, olive oil, salt, and pepper.
3. Pour the dressing over the quinoa salad and toss gently to combine.
4. Serve chilled or at room temperature.

Nutritional Facts (per serving):

Calories: 400
Protein: 12g
Carbs: 52g
Fat: 18g

Key Nutrients:

Fiber (quinoa, black beans)
Healthy fats (avocado)
Vitamin C (red bell pepper)

Tips:
Add a sprinkle of pumpkin seeds for extra zinc, a mineral essential for reproductive health.

12. Kale and Sweet Potato Salad with Tahini Dressing

This vibrant salad is rich in beta-carotene, folate, and antioxidants, all of which support hormone production and egg quality.

Prep Time: 15 minutes
Cooking Time: 25 minutes
Servings: 2

Ingredients:

- 2 cups chopped kale
- 1 medium sweet potato, diced and roasted
- 1/4 cup pomegranate seeds
- 1/4 cup chickpeas, rinsed and drained
- 2 tablespoons tahini
- Juice of 1 lemon
- 1 tablespoon olive oil
- Salt and pepper to taste

Instructions:

1. Preheat the oven to 400°F (200°C). Toss the diced sweet potato with olive oil, salt, and pepper. Spread on a baking sheet and roast for 20-25 minutes, or until tender.
2. In a large bowl, massage the chopped kale with lemon juice and a pinch of salt to soften.
3. Add the roasted sweet potato, pomegranate seeds, and chickpeas to the kale.
4. In a small bowl, whisk together tahini, lemon juice, olive oil, salt, and pepper.
5. Drizzle the tahini dressing over the salad and toss to combine.

Nutritional Facts (per serving):

Calories: 380
Protein: 10g
Carbs: 52g
Fat: 16g

Key Nutrients:

Beta-carotene (sweet potatoes)
Folate (kale)
Antioxidants (pomegranate seeds)

Tips:
For added protein, top with grilled chicken or a boiled egg.

13. Grilled Vegetable and Hummus Wrap

This wrap is loaded with plant-based protein and antioxidants, promoting gut health and reducing inflammation.

Prep Time: 10 minutes
Cooking Time: 7 minutes
Servings: 1

Ingredients:

- 1 whole-grain tortilla
- 1/2 cup hummus
- 1/4 cup sliced bell peppers (red, yellow, or green)
- 1/4 cup sliced zucchini
- 1/4 cup sliced red onion
- 1 tablespoon olive oil
- Salt and pepper to taste
- Handful of mixed greens

Instructions:

1. Heat olive oil in a skillet over medium heat. Add sliced bell peppers, zucchini, and red onion. Season with salt and pepper, and sauté for 5-7 minutes, or until tender.
2. Spread hummus evenly over the whole-grain tortilla.
3. Layer the grilled vegetables on top of the hummus and add mixed greens.
4. Roll the tortilla tightly, slice in half, and serve.

Nutritional Facts (per serving):

Calories: 360
Protein: 12g
Carbs: 45g
Fat: 16g

Key Nutrients:

Fiber (hummus, vegetables)
Healthy fats (olive oil)
Antioxidants (bell peppers)

Tips:
For a protein boost, add grilled chicken or tofu to the wrap.

14. Lemon Herb Chicken and Farro Salad

This salad combines lean protein, whole grains, and fresh vegetables, supporting hormone regulation and stable blood sugar levels.

Prep Time: 15 minutes
Cooking Time: 25 minutes
Servings: 2

Ingredients:

- 1 cup cooked farro
- 1 grilled chicken breast, sliced
- 1/2 cup cherry tomatoes, halved
- 1/4 cup diced cucumber
- 1/4 cup chopped parsley
- 2 tablespoons crumbled feta cheese
- Juice of 1 lemon
- 1 tablespoon olive oil
- Salt and pepper to taste

Instructions:

1. In a large bowl, combine cooked farro, sliced grilled chicken, cherry tomatoes, cucumber, parsley, and feta cheese.
2. In a small bowl, whisk together lemon juice, olive oil, salt, and pepper.
3. Pour the dressing over the salad and toss to combine.
4. Serve chilled or at room temperature.

Nutritional Facts (per serving):

Calories: 450
Protein: 30g
Carbs: 52g
Fat: 16g

Key Nutrients:

Protein (chicken)
Complex carbohydrates (farro)
Antioxidants (parsley, tomatoes)

Tips:
Add a handful of arugula or spinach for extra greens.

15. Eggplant and Chickpea Stew

This hearty stew is rich in plant-based protein, fiber, and anti-inflammatory spices, all of which support hormone balance and overall reproductive health.

Prep Time: 10 minutes
Cooking Time: 30 minutes
Servings: 4

Ingredients:

- 1 medium eggplant, diced
- 1 can (14 oz) chickpeas, rinsed and drained
- 1 can (14 oz) diced tomatoes
- 1 onion, diced
- 2 garlic cloves, minced
- 1 teaspoon cumin
- 1 teaspoon smoked paprika
- 1 tablespoon olive oil
- Salt and pepper to taste
- Fresh parsley for garnish

Instructions:

1. Heat olive oil in a large pot over medium heat. Add the diced onion and minced garlic, sautéing until fragrant (about 3 minutes).
2. Add the diced eggplant, cumin, and smoked paprika. Cook for 5-7 minutes, stirring occasionally.
3. Stir in chickpeas and diced tomatoes. Bring the mixture to a simmer and cook for 20 minutes, stirring occasionally.
4. Season with salt and pepper, and garnish with fresh parsley before serving.

Nutritional Facts (per serving):

Calories: 340
Protein: 12g
Carbs: 48g
Fat: 12g

Key Nutrients:

Fiber (chickpeas, eggplant)
Antioxidants (tomatoes, spices)
Plant-based protein (chickpeas)

Tips:
Serve with whole-grain bread or brown rice to make it a complete meal.

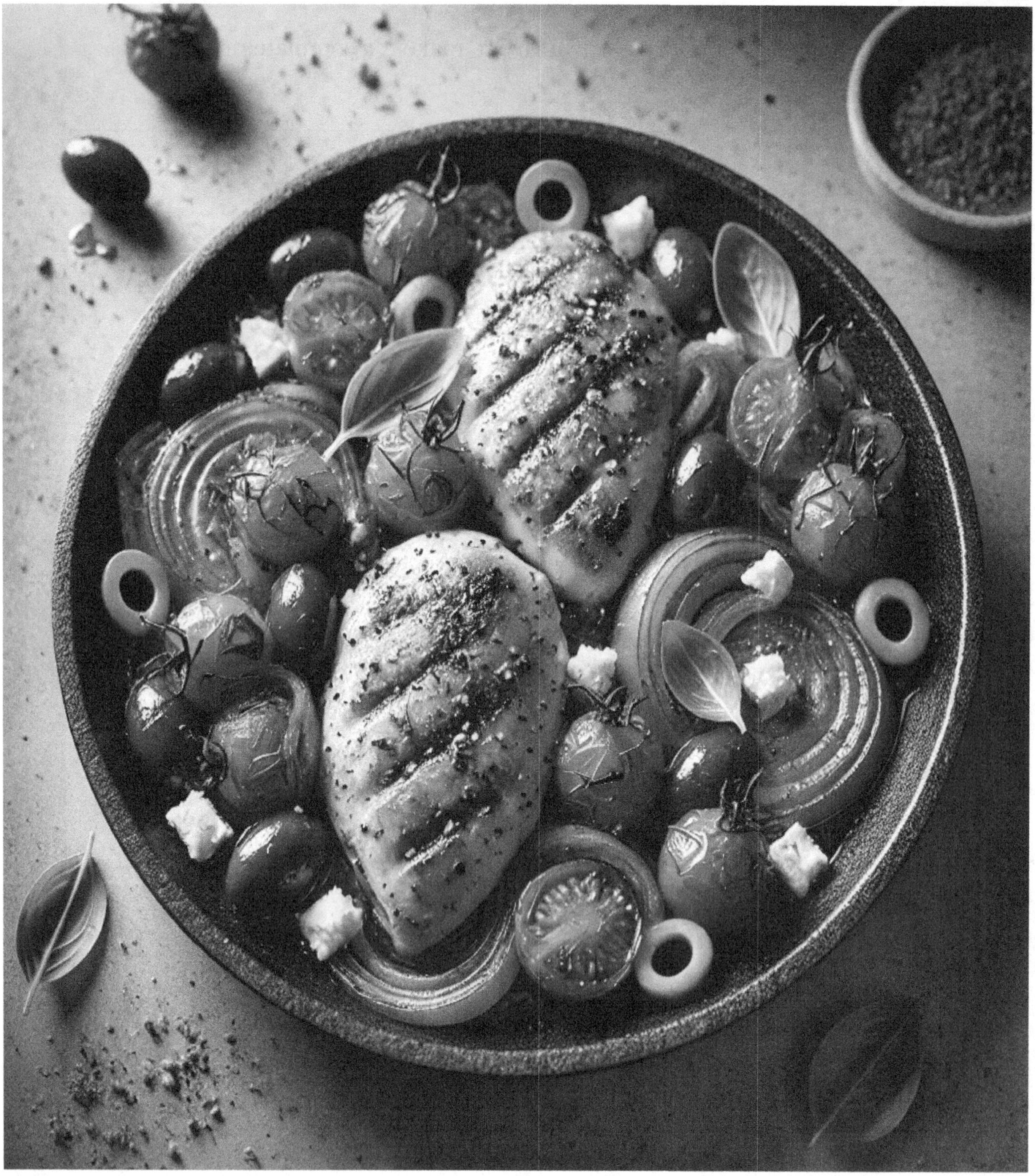

Chapter 5 Dinners for Two

Evening meals hold a unique place in our daily routines—a time when the pace of the day slows, and the focus shifts to nourishment, connection, and reflection. For couples on a fertility journey, dinner can become a powerful ritual of care and intention, offering not just sustenance but a meaningful way to align your lifestyle with your shared goals. It's a moment to turn the simple act of eating into an opportunity to prioritize your health and your relationship, laying the groundwork for a stronger future together.

From the ingredients you choose to the experience of cooking and eating together, dinner can significantly impact both physical and emotional well-being. Fertility-supportive meals are about more than just calories; they are carefully designed to deliver the essential nutrients your body needs to thrive. This chapter features recipes packed with hormone-balancing fats, cell-protecting antioxidants, and high-quality proteins—all essential for enhancing reproductive health. Each dish is crafted to nourish egg and sperm quality, support a healthy hormonal balance, and promote overall vitality.

Sharing a dinner as a couple does more than feed the body—it nurtures the bond between you. Cooking together encourages collaboration and teamwork, transforming the kitchen into a space of connection. Research has shown that shared meals strengthen relationships, and this becomes even more significant during the fertility journey. These recipes are tailored for two, making it easy to create a special, intimate dining experience while ensuring both partners benefit from the nutrient-packed dishes.

Dinners also offer a chance to unwind and reset. After the challenges of the day, the act of sitting down to a wholesome, homemade meal can provide a sense of calm and gratitude. Stress is a known disruptor of fertility, and these recipes not only deliver the nutrients needed to combat inflammation and oxidative stress but also encourage mindful eating practices that soothe the mind. By taking the time to slow down and savor your meal, you are actively creating a more supportive environment for conception.

In this chapter, you'll find a variety of delicious, fertility-focused dinner options—from hearty one-pan meals to elegant seafood dishes and comforting vegetarian bowls. These recipes are as flavorful as they are nourishing, designed to satisfy your taste buds while delivering powerful benefits to your reproductive health. Whether it's the omega-3s in wild-caught salmon, the fiber in roasted root vegetables, or the zinc in lean cuts of beef, every ingredient is chosen to support your journey in a meaningful way.

Let dinner become a nightly celebration of your commitment to this chapter of your life. With every meal, you're not only feeding your bodies but also cultivating an environment of love, care, and shared purpose. These recipes will guide you in creating meals that satisfy your hunger, nurture your health, and bring you closer to your ultimate goal of parenthood.

1. Lemon Herb Salmon with Asparagus

Salmon is rich in omega-3 fatty acids, which improve egg and sperm quality, while asparagus provides folate, crucial for reproductive health.

Prep Time: 10 minutes
Cooking Time: 20 minutes
Servings: 2

Ingredients:

- 2 salmon fillets (6 oz each)
- 1 bunch asparagus, trimmed
- 2 tablespoons olive oil
- Juice of 1 lemon
- 2 garlic cloves, minced
- Salt and pepper
- Fresh dill for garnish

Instructions:

1. Preheat the oven to 400°F (200°C) and line a baking sheet with parchment paper.
2. Arrange the salmon fillets and asparagus on the baking sheet.
3. Drizzle with olive oil and lemon juice, then sprinkle with minced garlic, salt, and pepper.
4. Roast for 15-20 minutes until the salmon is flaky and the asparagus is tender.
5. Garnish with fresh dill before serving.

Nutritional Facts (per serving):

Calories: 450
Protein: 34g
Carbs: 10g
Fat: 28g

Key Nutrients:

Omega-3 fatty acids (salmon)
Folate (asparagus)
Antioxidants (lemon and garlic)

Tips:
Serve with a side of quinoa or wild rice for a balanced meal.

2. Crispy Ground Beef Stuffed Bell Peppers

This dish delivers iron, zinc, and vitamin C, supporting hormone balance and reducing oxidative stress.

Prep Time: 10 minutes
Cooking Time: 40 minutes
Servings: 2

Ingredients:

- 2 large bell peppers, halved and seeds removed
- 1 cup cooked ground beef (seasoned)
- 1/2 cup diced tomatoes
- 1/4 cup corn kernels (canned or fresh)
- 1/4 cup grated Parmesan cheese
- 1 teaspoon cumin
- Salt and pepper
- Fresh cilantro for garnish

Instructions:

1. Preheat the oven to 375°F (190°C) and line a baking dish with parchment paper.
2. In a bowl, mix ground beef, diced tomatoes, corn, cumin, salt, and pepper.
3. Stuff the bell pepper halves with the beef mixture and place them in the dish.
4. Top with Parmesan cheese, cover with foil, and bake for 25 minutes. Remove the foil and bake for another 10-15 minutes until golden brown.
5. Garnish with cilantro before serving.

Nutritional Facts (per serving):

Calories: 380
Protein: 24g
Carbs: 18g
Fat: 24g

Key Nutrients:

Iron (beef)
Vitamin C (bell peppers)
Folate (tomatoes)

Tips:
For a vegetarian option, replace beef with lentils or black beans.

3. Garlic Shrimp and Zucchini Noodles

Shrimp supplies selenium for sperm health, while zucchini noodles are low-carb and nutrient-dense, aiding hormonal balance.

Prep Time: 10 minutes
Cooking Time: 10 minutes
Servings: 2

Ingredients:

- 12 large shrimp, peeled and deveined
- 2 medium zucchini, spiralized
- 2 tablespoons olive oil
- 3 garlic cloves, minced
- Juice of 1 lemon
- Salt and pepper
- Red pepper flakes (optional)
- Fresh parsley for garnish

Instructions:

1. Heat olive oil in a skillet over medium heat. Add garlic and cook for 1 minute.
2. Add shrimp and cook for 2-3 minutes per side until pink. Remove and set aside.
3. Add zucchini noodles to the skillet and sauté for 2-3 minutes.
4. Return shrimp to the skillet, add lemon juice, salt, and pepper, and toss to combine.
5. Garnish with parsley and serve hot.

Nutritional Facts (per serving):

Calories: 320
Protein: 26g
Carbs: 10g
Fat: 18g

Key Nutrients:

Selenium (shrimp)
Vitamin C (lemon)
Fiber (zucchini)

Tips:
Top with a sprinkle of Parmesan for added flavor.

4. Mediterranean Chicken Skillet

Packed with lean protein and antioxidants, this dish supports hormone production and reduces inflammation.

Prep Time: 10 minutes
Cooking Time: 15 minutes
Servings: 2

Ingredients:

- 2 chicken breasts
- 1/2 cup cherry tomatoes, halved
- 1/4 cup Kalamata olives
- 1/4 cup diced red onion
- 1/4 cup feta cheese
- 2 tablespoons olive oil
- 1 teaspoon dried oregano
- Salt and pepper
- Fresh basil for garnish

Instructions:

1. Heat olive oil in a skillet over medium heat. Season chicken with oregano, salt, and pepper.
2. Cook chicken for 6-7 minutes per side until golden brown and fully cooked.
3. Add cherry tomatoes, olives, and red onion to the skillet, cooking for 3-4 minutes.
4. Sprinkle feta cheese over the top and garnish with basil before serving.

Nutritional Facts (per serving):

Calories: 450
Protein: 36g
Carbs: 12g
Fat: 28g

Key Nutrients:

Lean protein (chicken)
Healthy fats (olives, olive oil)
Antioxidants (tomatoes)

Tips:
Serve with a side of couscous or whole-grain pita bread.

5. Butternut Squash and Spinach Risotto

This creamy risotto is rich in beta-carotene and folate, crucial for hormonal balance and egg quality.

Prep Time: 10 minutes
Cooking Time: 30 minutes
Servings: 2

Ingredients:

- 1 cup Arborio rice
- 2 cups diced butternut squash
- 2 cups spinach leaves
- 1/2 onion, diced
- 3 cups vegetable broth
- 1/4 cup grated Parmesan cheese
- 2 tablespoons olive oil
- Salt and pepper

Instructions:

1. Heat olive oil in a pan over medium heat. Sauté onion for 5 minutes.
2. Add butternut squash and cook for another 5 minutes.
3. Stir in Arborio rice and cook for 2 minutes. Gradually add vegetable broth, one cup at a time, stirring until absorbed.
4. Add spinach and Parmesan, stirring until creamy. Season with salt and pepper.
5. Serve hot.

Nutritional Facts (per serving):

Calories: 420
Protein: 12g
Carbs: 65g
Fat: 12g

Key Nutrients:

Beta-carotene (butternut squash)
Folate (spinach)
Calcium (Parmesan)

Tips:
Add grilled shrimp or chicken for extra protein.

6. Penne Bolognese

This hearty dish combines iron-rich ground beef and whole-grain pasta, supporting hormone production and stabilizing blood sugar.

Prep Time: 10 minutes
Cooking Time: 2 hours
Servings: 4

Ingredients:

- 12 oz whole-grain penne pasta
- 1 pound ground beef
- 1 small onion, diced
- 1 carrot, finely diced
- 1 celery stalk, finely diced
- 1 can (14 oz) diced tomatoes
- 1/4 cup tomato paste
- 1/2 cup red wine (optional)
- 2 tablespoons olive oil
- Salt and pepper to taste
- 1/4 cup grated Parmesan cheese (for serving)

Instructions:

1. Bring a large pot of salted water to a boil. Cook penne according to package instructions until al dente. Drain and set aside.
2. Heat olive oil in a large skillet over medium heat. Add onion, carrot, and celery. Cook for 5 minutes, until softened.
3. Add ground beef and cook until browned, breaking it up with a spoon.
4. Stir in tomato paste and diced tomatoes. If using, add red wine and simmer for 90-100 minutes, stirring occasionally, until thickened.
5. Toss the cooked pasta with the Bolognese sauce.
6. Serve hot, topped with grated Parmesan cheese.

Nutritional Facts (per serving):

Calories: 460
Protein: 28g
Carbs: 45g
Fat: 16g

Key Nutrients:

Iron (ground beef)
Fiber (whole-grain pasta)
Lycopene (tomatoes)

Tips:
For extra flavor, add fresh basil or oregano before serving.

---

7. Baked Cod with Garlic and Herbs

Cod is rich in lean protein and omega-3s, supporting egg and sperm health. Garlic and herbs boost antioxidants.

Prep Time: 10 minutes
Cooking Time: 15 minutes
Servings: 2

Ingredients:

- 2 cod fillets (6 oz each)
- 3 garlic cloves, minced
- 1 tablespoon fresh parsley, chopped
- 1 tablespoon fresh dill, chopped
- 2 tablespoons olive oil
- Juice of 1 lemon
- Salt and pepper

Instructions:

1. Preheat the oven to 375°F (190°C). Line a baking dish with parchment paper.
2. Arrange the cod fillets in the dish. Drizzle with olive oil and lemon juice.
3. Sprinkle minced garlic, parsley, dill, salt, and pepper over the fillets.
4. Bake for 15-20 minutes, until the fish flakes easily with a fork.
5. Serve with steamed green beans or roasted asparagus.

Nutritional Facts (per serving):

Calories: 310
Protein: 32g
Carbs: 4g
Fat: 18g

Key Nutrients:

Omega-3s (cod)
Vitamin C (lemon)
Antioxidants (herbs)

Tips:
Add a side of quinoa or wild rice for a more complete meal.

---

8. Cauliflower Fried Rice with Shrimp

This low-carb dish is rich in selenium and choline, supporting reproductive cell health and egg quality.

Prep Time: 15 minutes
Cooking Time: 15 minutes
Servings: 2

Ingredients:

- 2 cups riced cauliflower
- 12 large shrimp, peeled and deveined
- 1/2 cup diced carrots
- 1/4 cup green peas
- 2 garlic cloves, minced
- 2 eggs, beaten
- 2 tablespoons soy sauce (or tamari for gluten-free)
- 1 tablespoon sesame oil
- 2 green onions, chopped
- Salt and pepper

Instructions:

1. Heat sesame oil in a large skillet over medium heat. Add garlic and cook for 1 minute until fragrant.
2. Add shrimp and cook for 2-3 minutes per side until pink. Remove shrimp and set aside.
3. Add riced cauliflower, carrots, and peas to the skillet. Cook for 5-7 minutes, stirring frequently.
4. Push the vegetables to one side and scramble the beaten eggs in the empty space.
5. Stir in shrimp, soy sauce, salt, and pepper. Top with green onions before serving.

Nutritional Facts (per serving):

Calories: 350
Protein: 28g
Carbs: 20g
Fat: 18g

Key Nutrients:

Selenium (shrimp)
Fiber (cauliflower)
Choline (eggs)

Tips:
Swap shrimp with tofu for a vegetarian option.

9. Stuffed Portobello Mushrooms with Spinach and Goat Cheese

Portobello mushrooms are a great source of vitamin D, while spinach provides folate for cell division.

Prep Time: 10 minutes
Cooking Time: 20 minutes
Servings: 2

Ingredients:

- 4 large Portobello mushrooms, stems removed
- 2 cups fresh spinach
- 1/2 cup goat cheese
- 1/4 cup sun-dried tomatoes, chopped
- 2 garlic cloves, minced
- 2 tablespoons olive oil
- Salt and pepper
- Fresh basil for garnish

Instructions:

1. Preheat the oven to 375°F (190°C). Brush mushrooms with olive oil and season with salt and pepper. Arrange on a baking sheet.
2. Heat olive oil in a skillet over medium heat. Add garlic and spinach, cooking until wilted.
3. Mix in goat cheese and sun-dried tomatoes. Spoon the mixture into the mushroom caps.
4. Bake for 15-20 minutes until the mushrooms are tender.
5. Garnish with fresh basil and serve hot.

Nutritional Facts (per serving):

Calories: 320
Protein: 12g
Carbs: 16g
Fat: 26g

Key Nutrients:

Vitamin D (mushrooms)
Folate (spinach)
Calcium (goat cheese)

Tips:
Serve alongside a simple green salad for a complete meal.

10. Beef and Broccoli Stir-Fry

This stir-fry is rich in zinc and iron, promoting ovulation and sperm health, while broccoli provides antioxidants.

Prep Time: 10 minutes
Cooking Time: 15 minutes
Servings: 2

Ingredients:

- 8 oz flank steak, thinly sliced
- 2 cups broccoli florets
- 1 red bell pepper, sliced
- 2 garlic cloves, minced
- 2 tablespoons soy sauce (or tamari)
- 1 tablespoon oyster sauce
- 1 tablespoon sesame oil
- 1 teaspoon grated ginger
- Sesame seeds for garnish

Instructions:

1. Heat sesame oil in a skillet over medium-high heat. Add garlic and ginger, cooking for 1 minute.
2. Add sliced steak and cook for 3-4 minutes until browned.
3. Add broccoli and bell pepper, stirring frequently, and cook for 5-7 minutes.
4. Stir in soy sauce and oyster sauce, cooking for 2 more minutes.
5. Garnish with sesame seeds and serve hot.

Nutritional Facts (per serving):

Calories: 420
Protein: 28g
Carbs: 20g
Fat: 26g

Key Nutrients:

Zinc (beef)
Vitamin C (broccoli)
Antioxidants (bell pepper)

Tips:
Serve over brown rice or quinoa for added fiber and nutrients.

11. Chicken and Butternut Squash Sheet Pan Dinner

This nutrient-dense dish combines lean protein and beta-carotene-rich squash to support egg quality and hormonal health.

Prep Time: 10 minutes
Cooking Time: 30 minutes
Servings: 2

Ingredients:

- 2 boneless, skinless chicken breasts
- 2 cups butternut squash, diced
- 1 red onion, sliced
- 1 tablespoon olive oil
- 1 teaspoon dried rosemary
- 1 teaspoon dried thyme
- Salt and pepper
- Fresh parsley for garnish

Instructions:

1. Preheat the oven to 400°F (200°C). Line a baking sheet with parchment paper.
2. Toss the diced butternut squash and red onion with olive oil, rosemary, thyme, salt, and pepper.
3. Place the chicken breasts on the baking sheet and season with salt and pepper. Arrange the squash and onion around the chicken.
4. Roast for 25-30 minutes until the chicken is cooked through and the squash is tender.
5. Garnish with fresh parsley before serving.

Nutritional Facts (per serving):

Calories: 450
Protein: 34g
Carbs: 30g
Fat: 20g

Key Nutrients:

Beta-carotene (butternut squash)
Lean protein (chicken)
Antioxidants (red onion)

Tips:
For extra flavor, marinate the chicken in lemon juice and garlic before roasting.

12. Spicy Chickpea and Spinach Curry

Chickpeas and spinach provide folate, protein, and iron, which are essential for reproductive health.

Prep Time: 10 minutes
Cooking Time: 20 minutes
Servings: 4

Ingredients:

- 1 can (14 oz) chickpeas, rinsed and drained
- 2 cups fresh spinach
- 1 onion, diced
- 2 garlic cloves, minced
- 1 can (14 oz) coconut milk
- 1 tablespoon curry powder
- 1 teaspoon turmeric
- 1/2 teaspoon chili flakes
- 2 tablespoons olive oil
- Salt and pepper
- Fresh cilantro for garnish

Instructions:

1. Heat olive oil in a large pan over medium heat. Add onion and garlic, sautéing until softened.
2. Stir in curry powder, turmeric, and chili flakes. Cook for 1 minute until fragrant.
3. Add chickpeas and coconut milk. Simmer for 10-15 minutes to allow the flavors to meld.
4. Stir in spinach and cook until wilted. Season with salt and pepper.
5. Garnish with fresh cilantro and serve hot with brown rice or quinoa.

Nutritional Facts (per serving):

Calories: 400
Protein: 12g
Carbs: 40g
Fat: 22g

Key Nutrients:

Folate (spinach)
Iron (chickpeas)
Healthy fats (coconut milk)

Tips:
Adjust the spice level by increasing or reducing the chili flakes.

---

13. Zesty Lemon and Garlic Shrimp Pasta

This dish provides zinc, antioxidants, and fiber to support reproductive health and stable blood sugar.

Prep Time: 10 minutes
Cooking Time: 15 minutes
Servings: 2

Ingredients:

- 8 oz whole-grain spaghetti
- 12 large shrimp, peeled and deveined
- 3 garlic cloves, minced
- Juice of 1 lemon
- 2 tablespoons olive oil
- 1/4 teaspoon red pepper flakes
- Salt and pepper
- Fresh parsley for garnish

Instructions:

1. Cook the whole-grain spaghetti according to package instructions. Drain and set aside.
2. Heat olive oil in a skillet over medium heat. Add garlic and red pepper flakes, cooking for 1 minute.
3. Add shrimp and cook for 2-3 minutes per side until pink and opaque.
4. Stir in cooked spaghetti and lemon juice. Toss to combine.
5. Garnish with fresh parsley and serve hot.

Nutritional Facts (per serving):

Calories: 450
Protein: 28g
Carbs: 50g
Fat: 18g

Key Nutrients:

Zinc (shrimp)
Fiber (whole-grain pasta)
Vitamin C (lemon)

Tips:
Substitute zucchini noodles for a lower-carb option.

---

14. Eggplant Parmesan for Two

Eggplant is high in fiber and antioxidants, supporting gut and hormone health, while cheese provides calcium and protein.

Prep Time: 15 minutes
Cooking Time: 25 minutes
Servings: 2

Ingredients:

- 1 medium eggplant, sliced into rounds
- 1/2 cup whole-wheat breadcrumbs
- 1/4 cup grated Parmesan cheese
- 1 egg, beaten
- 1 cup marinara sauce
- 1/2 cup shredded mozzarella cheese
- 1 tablespoon olive oil
- Fresh basil for garnish

Instructions:

1. Preheat the oven to 375°F (190°C). Line a baking sheet with parchment paper.
2. Dip eggplant slices into beaten egg, then coat with breadcrumbs mixed with Parmesan cheese.
3. Heat olive oil in a skillet and fry the eggplant slices until golden brown on both sides.
4. Place fried eggplant slices in a baking dish. Top with marinara sauce and mozzarella cheese.
5. Bake for 15-20 minutes until the cheese is bubbly. Garnish with fresh basil.

Nutritional Facts (per serving):

Calories: 420
Protein: 18g
Carbs: 42g
Fat: 22g

Key Nutrients:

Fiber (eggplant)
Calcium (cheese)
Lycopene (marinara sauce)

Tips:
Pair with a side salad for added greens.

15. One-Pan Lemon Herb Chicken and Broccoli

This one-pan dish is packed with lean protein, zinc, and antioxidants, which support reproductive health.

Prep Time: 10 minutes
Cooking Time: 30 minutes
Servings: 2

Ingredients:

- 2 chicken thighs, bone-in, skin-on
- 2 cups broccoli florets
- 1 lemon, sliced
- 3 garlic cloves, minced
- 2 tablespoons olive oil
- 1 teaspoon dried thyme
- Salt and pepper

Instructions:

1. Preheat the oven to 400°F (200°C). Line a baking sheet with parchment paper.
2. In a bowl, mix olive oil, garlic, thyme, salt, and pepper. Rub this mixture onto the chicken thighs.
3. Place the chicken thighs on the baking sheet and arrange the broccoli and lemon slices around them.
4. Roast for 30-35 minutes, until the chicken skin is crispy and the broccoli is tender.
5. Serve hot, drizzled with any leftover pan juices.

Nutritional Facts (per serving):

Calories: 450
Protein: 28g
Carbs: 12g
Fat: 30g

Key Nutrients:

Zinc (chicken)
Vitamin C (broccoli)
Antioxidants (lemon)

Tips:
Add a sprinkle of red pepper flakes for a spicy kick.

16. Basil Pesto Chicken with Roasted Vegetables

Basil pesto is packed with healthy fats and antioxidants, supporting hormone production and reducing inflammation.

Prep Time: 10 minutes
Cooking Time: 25 minutes
Servings: 2

Ingredients:

- 2 boneless, skinless chicken breasts
- 1/4 cup basil pesto (store-bought or homemade)
- 1 cup cherry tomatoes
- 1 cup sliced zucchini
- 1 red bell pepper, sliced
- 2 tablespoons olive oil
- Salt and pepper
- Fresh basil leaves for garnish

Instructions:

1. Preheat the oven to 400°F (200°C). Line a baking sheet with parchment paper.
2. Coat the chicken breasts with basil pesto and place them on one side of the baking sheet.
3. Toss the cherry tomatoes, zucchini, and red bell pepper slices with olive oil, salt, and pepper. Arrange the vegetables on the other side of the baking sheet.
4. Roast for 20-25 minutes, or until the chicken is fully cooked and the vegetables are tender.
5. Garnish with fresh basil leaves and serve hot.

Nutritional Facts (per serving):

Calories: 430
Protein: 32g
Carbs: 16g
Fat: 28g

Key Nutrients:

Antioxidants (basil, tomatoes, bell peppers)
Lean protein (chicken)
Healthy fats (pesto, olive oil)

Tips:
For added flavor, sprinkle the vegetables with a pinch of Italian seasoning before roasting.

17. Honey Garlic Glazed Salmon

Rich in omega-3 fatty acids, this salmon dish supports egg and sperm quality while reducing inflammation.

Prep Time: 5 minutes
Cooking Time: 10 minutes
Servings: 2

Ingredients:

- 2 salmon fillets (6 oz each)
- 2 tablespoons honey
- 2 garlic cloves, minced
- 2 tablespoons soy sauce (or tamari for gluten-free)
- 1 tablespoon lemon juice
- 1 tablespoon olive oil
- Salt and pepper
- Fresh chives for garnish

Instructions:

1. In a small bowl, mix honey, garlic, soy sauce, lemon juice, and olive oil.
2. Heat a skillet over medium heat and add the salmon fillets, skin-side down. Cook for 3-4 minutes.
3. Flip the salmon and pour the honey garlic glaze over the fillets. Cook for another 2-3 minutes, allowing the glaze to caramelize.
4. Garnish with fresh chives and serve hot with steamed vegetables or rice.

Nutritional Facts (per serving):

Calories: 420
Protein: 30g
Carbs: 18g
Fat: 24g

Key Nutrients:

Omega-3s (salmon)
Antioxidants (garlic)
Vitamin C (lemon)

Tips:
For an extra touch of flavor, add a pinch of red pepper flakes to the glaze.

18. Beef and Sweet Potato Skillet

This hearty skillet provides iron, zinc, and beta-carotene, essential for ovulation and hormone regulation.

Prep Time: 10 minutes
Cooking Time: 25 minutes
Servings: 2

Ingredients:

- 1/2 pound lean ground beef
- 1 medium sweet potato, diced
- 1/2 onion, diced
- 1 red bell pepper, diced
- 2 garlic cloves, minced
- 2 tablespoons olive oil
- 1 teaspoon smoked paprika
- Salt and pepper
- Fresh parsley for garnish

Instructions:

1. Heat olive oil in a skillet over medium heat. Add onion and garlic, sautéing until fragrant.
2. Add ground beef, cooking until browned and breaking it up with a spoon.
3. Stir in diced sweet potato and red bell pepper. Season with smoked paprika, salt, and pepper.
4. Cover the skillet and cook for 10-15 minutes, stirring occasionally, until the sweet potato is tender.
5. Garnish with fresh parsley and serve hot.

Nutritional Facts (per serving):

Calories: 450
Protein: 28g
Carbs: 36g
Fat: 22g

Key Nutrients:

Beta-carotene (sweet potato)
Iron and zinc (beef)
Vitamin C (bell pepper)

Tips:
Add a splash of Worcestershire sauce for a savory depth of flavor.

---

19. Vegetarian Lentil Bolognese

Lentils offer plant-based protein and iron, which support cell division and ovulation.

Prep Time: 10 minutes
Cooking Time: 30 minutes
Servings: 4

Ingredients:

- 1 cup dried lentils, rinsed
- 1 can (14 oz) diced tomatoes
- 1/2 onion, diced
- 2 garlic cloves, minced
- 1 carrot, diced
- 1 celery stalk, diced
- 1 tablespoon olive oil
- 1 teaspoon dried oregano
- 1 teaspoon dried basil
- Salt and pepper
- 8 oz whole-grain spaghetti

Instructions:

1. Cook the lentils according to package instructions. Drain and set aside.
2. In a large pan, heat olive oil over medium heat. Sauté onion, garlic, carrot, and celery until softened.
3. Add diced tomatoes, oregano, basil, salt, and pepper. Stir in the cooked lentils.
4. Simmer the sauce for 15-20 minutes, allowing it to thicken.
5. Cook the whole-grain spaghetti according to package instructions. Drain and toss with the lentil Bolognese sauce.
6. Serve hot, garnished with fresh basil.

Nutritional Facts (per serving):

Calories: 460
Protein: 20g
Carbs: 68g
Fat: 12g

Key Nutrients:

Plant-based protein (lentils)
Fiber (whole-grain pasta)
Antioxidants (tomatoes)

Tips:
Use zucchini noodles for a lower-carb option.

---

20. Sesame Ginger Tofu Stir-Fry

Tofu provides plant-based protein and phytoestrogens, which promote hormonal health.

Prep Time: 10 minutes
Cooking Time: 15 minutes
Servings: 2

Ingredients:

- 8 oz firm tofu, pressed and cubed
- 2 cups mixed vegetables (broccoli, bell peppers, snap peas)
- 2 garlic cloves, minced
- 1 tablespoon grated ginger
- 2 tablespoons soy sauce (or tamari)
- 1 tablespoon sesame oil
- 1 tablespoon honey
- 1 teaspoon cornstarch (optional, for thickening)
- Sesame seeds for garnish
- Fresh green onions for garnish

Instructions:

1. Heat sesame oil in a skillet over medium-high heat. Add tofu cubes and cook until golden brown on all sides. Remove and set aside.
2. In the same skillet, add garlic, ginger, and mixed vegetables. Stir-fry for 5-7 minutes until tender.
3. In a small bowl, mix soy sauce, honey, and cornstarch (if using). Pour the sauce into the skillet.
4. Return the tofu to the skillet and toss everything together until coated.
5. Garnish with sesame seeds and green onions before serving.

Nutritional Facts (per serving):

Calories: 380
Protein: 18g
Carbs: 30g
Fat: 20g

Key Nutrients:

Plant-based protein (tofu)
Antioxidants (ginger, vegetables)
Zinc (sesame seeds)

Tips:
Serve over brown rice or quinoa for a complete meal.

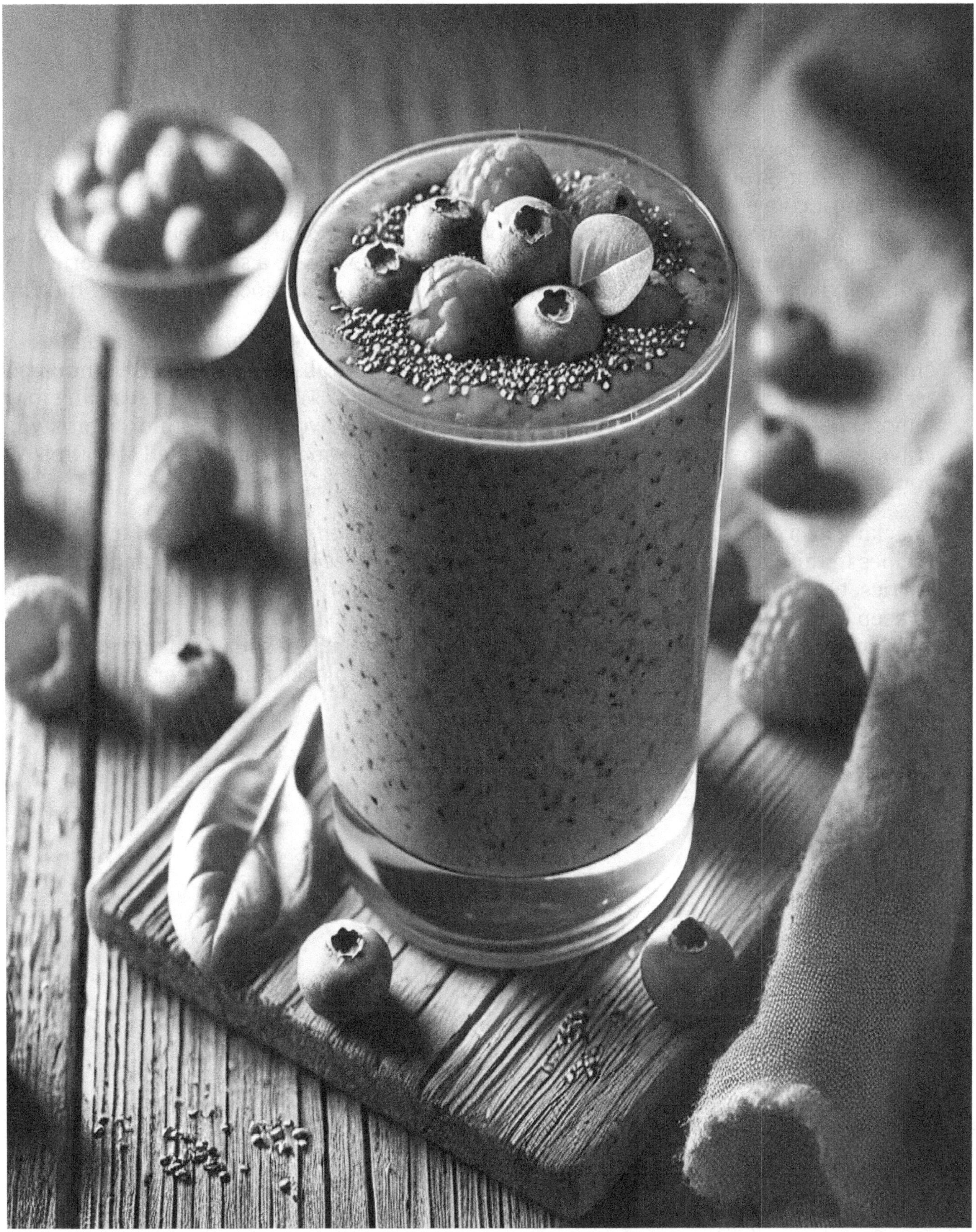

Chapter 6 Snacks and Smoothies

Snacking is more than just a way to fill the gaps between meals—it's a chance to nourish your body and provide consistent energy to support your fertility journey. The right snacks are not just convenient; they're an essential part of maintaining hormonal balance, stabilizing blood sugar, and fueling your body with the key nutrients needed to enhance reproductive health. When chosen thoughtfully, snacks can be a simple yet powerful way to reduce inflammation, improve energy levels, and sustain your focus throughout the day.

This section brings you a carefully curated selection of nutrient-packed snacks and smoothies designed with fertility in mind. From quick, grab-and-go options to indulgent treats, these recipes are as practical as they are beneficial. Whether you're reaching for a handful of fertility-boosting trail mix, enjoying a creamy avocado smoothie, or satisfying a craving with antioxidant-rich dark chocolate bark, these snacks are crafted to complement your main meals and keep you on track toward your goals.

Snacking also offers an opportunity to address specific nutritional needs. Many of the recipes in this chapter feature ingredients like nuts and seeds, rich in zinc and healthy fats; berries, bursting with antioxidants to combat oxidative stress; and protein-packed options to keep hunger at bay while supporting egg and sperm health. These snacks not only satisfy your cravings but also deliver vital nutrients like folate, magnesium, and omega-3s, ensuring your body is constantly receiving the building blocks it needs for optimal fertility.

1. Fertility Trail Mix

This mix combines healthy fats, zinc, and antioxidants, which help support hormone production, egg quality, and sperm health.

Prep Time: 5 minutes
Cooking Time: None
Servings: 2

Ingredients:

- 1/4 cup almonds
- 1/4 cup walnuts
- 2 tablespoons pumpkin seeds
- 2 tablespoons sunflower seeds
- 2 tablespoons dried cranberries (unsweetened)
- 2 tablespoons dark chocolate chips (70% or higher)

Instructions:

1. Combine all ingredients in a bowl and mix well.
2. Store in an airtight container for a quick, nutrient-packed snack.

Nutritional Facts (per serving):

Calories: 280
Protein: 8g
Carbs: 20g
Fat: 20g

Key Nutrients:

Zinc (pumpkin seeds, sunflower seeds)
Healthy fats (almonds, walnuts)
Antioxidants (dark chocolate, cranberries)

Tips:

Customize this mix with your favorite nuts and seeds, but opt for unsweetened and raw varieties for the best nutritional benefits.

2. Berry Blast Smoothie

Packed with antioxidants, folate, and omega-3s, this smoothie helps protect reproductive cells and supports hormone balance.

Prep Time: 5 minutes
Cooking Time: None
Servings: 1

Ingredients:

- 1 cup unsweetened almond milk
- 1 cup mixed berries (blueberries, raspberries, strawberries)
- 1 handful of spinach
- 1 tablespoon chia seeds
- 1 banana
- 1 scoop protein powder (optional)

Instructions:

1. Add all ingredients to a blender and blend until smooth.
2. Serve immediately for a refreshing, nutrient-rich drink.

Nutritional Facts (per serving):

Calories: 300
Protein: 10g
Carbs: 52g
Fat: 8g

Key Nutrients:

Antioxidants (berries)
Omega-3s (chia seeds)
Folate (spinach)

Tips:
For extra creaminess, add half an avocado or a tablespoon of almond butter.

3. Pumpkin Seed Energy Bites

These energy bites are rich in zinc, which boosts sperm health and supports ovulation, while providing healthy fats for hormone regulation.

Prep Time: 10 minutes
Cooking Time: None
Servings: 12 (bite-sized)

Ingredients:

- 1 cup rolled oats
- 1/2 cup almond butter
- 1/4 cup honey
- 1/4 cup pumpkin seeds
- 1/4 cup dark chocolate chips
- 1 teaspoon vanilla extract

Instructions:

1. In a bowl, mix all ingredients until well combined.
2. Roll the mixture into bite-sized balls and refrigerate for at least 30 minutes.
3. Store in an airtight container in the fridge for up to one week.

Nutritional Facts (per bite):

Calories: 150
Protein: 4g
Carbs: 18g
Fat: 8g

Key Nutrients:

Zinc (pumpkin seeds)
Healthy fats (almond butter)
Antioxidants (dark chocolate)

Tips:
For variety, add shredded coconut or flaxseeds for additional nutrients.

4. Avocado Chocolate Smoothie

Avocado delivers monounsaturated fats for hormone production, while cocoa provides antioxidants that protect reproductive cells.

Prep Time: 5 minutes
Cooking Time: None
Servings: 1

Ingredients:

- 1/2 avocado
- 1 cup unsweetened almond milk
- 1 tablespoon cocoa powder
- 1 tablespoon honey
- 1/2 teaspoon vanilla extract
- Ice cubes

Instructions:

1. Combine all ingredients in a blender and blend until smooth and creamy.
2. Serve chilled for a nutrient-packed treat.

Nutritional Facts (per serving):

Calories: 320
Protein: 6g
Carbs: 28g
Fat: 20g

Key Nutrients:

Monounsaturated fats (avocado)
Antioxidants (cocoa)
Vitamin E (almond milk)

Tips:
Top with cacao nibs or chia seeds for added crunch and nutrients.

5. Apple Slices with Almond Butter

Apples provide fiber and antioxidants, while almond butter offers healthy fats and vitamin E for hormonal support.

Prep Time: 5 minutes
Cooking Time: None
Servings: 1

Ingredients:

- 1 medium apple, sliced
- 2 tablespoons almond butter
- 1 teaspoon chia seeds (optional)

Instructions:

1. Spread almond butter over the apple slices.
2. Sprinkle chia seeds on top for added crunch and omega-3s.

Nutritional Facts (per serving):

Calories: 250
Protein: 6g
Carbs: 34g
Fat: 12g

Key Nutrients:

Fiber (apple)
Omega-3s (chia seeds)
Healthy fats (almond butter)

Tips:
For a warming twist, sprinkle cinnamon over the apples before serving.

6. Green Goddess Smoothie

This hydrating smoothie is rich in folate, iron, and antioxidants to support reproductive health and reduce inflammation.

Prep Time: 5 minutes
Cooking Time: None
Servings: 1

Ingredients:

- 1 cup coconut water
- 1 handful kale
- 1/2 cucumber
- 1/2 banana
- 1 tablespoon ground flaxseeds
- Juice of 1/2 lemon

Instructions:

1. Blend all ingredients until smooth.
2. Serve immediately for a refreshing drink.

Nutritional Facts (per serving):

Calories: 200
Protein: 4g
Carbs: 38g
Fat: 6g

Key Nutrients:

Folate (kale)
Hydration (coconut water)
Omega-3s (flaxseeds)

Tips:
Freeze your banana beforehand to create a creamier texture.

7. Dark Chocolate and Walnut Bark

Dark chocolate is a rich source of antioxidants that protect eggs and sperm from oxidative damage, while walnuts provide omega-3 fatty acids that enhance reproductive health.

Prep Time: 5 minutes
Cooking Time: 30 minutes (to chill)
Servings: 8 pieces

Ingredients:

- 1/2 cup dark chocolate (70% cocoa), melted
- 1/4 cup chopped walnuts
- 1 tablespoon chia seeds

Instructions:

1. Melt the dark chocolate in a microwave-safe bowl, stirring every 20-30 seconds to prevent burning.
2. Spread the melted chocolate evenly on a parchment-lined baking sheet.
3. Sprinkle chopped walnuts and chia seeds over the chocolate.
4. Refrigerate for 30 minutes or until the chocolate is firm.
5. Break into pieces and store in an airtight container in the fridge.

Nutritional Facts (per piece):

Calories: 180
Protein: 3g
Carbs: 12g
Fat: 14g

Key Nutrients:

Antioxidants (dark chocolate)
Omega-3s (walnuts, chia seeds)
Magnesium (dark chocolate)

Tips:
Swap walnuts for pecans or almonds for variety. Add a sprinkle of sea salt for a sweet-and-salty twist.

8. Berry Chia Pudding

Chia seeds are packed with omega-3s and fiber, helping to reduce inflammation and support hormone regulation. Berries deliver a boost of antioxidants to protect reproductive cells.

Prep Time: 5 minutes
Cooking Time: 4 hours (to set)
Servings: 2

Ingredients:

- 1/4 cup chia seeds
- 1 cup almond milk
- 1 tablespoon honey
- 1/2 cup mixed berries

Instructions:

1. In a bowl, whisk together chia seeds, almond milk, and honey until well combined.
2. Cover and refrigerate for at least 4 hours or overnight, allowing the chia seeds to absorb the liquid and form a pudding-like texture.
3. Stir before serving and top with mixed berries.

Nutritional Facts (per serving):

Calories: 250
Protein: 6g
Carbs: 36g
Fat: 10g

Key Nutrients:

Omega-3s (chia seeds)
Antioxidants (berries)
Calcium (almond milk)

Tips:
Layer the pudding with berries in a glass for a visually stunning dessert. Add a drizzle of almond butter for extra healthy fats.

9. Carrot and Hummus Snack Plate

Carrots provide beta-carotene, essential for hormone regulation, while hummus delivers plant-based protein and fiber to stabilize blood sugar levels. Pumpkin seeds add zinc for reproductive health.

Prep Time: 5 minutes
Cooking Time: None
Servings: 1

Ingredients:

- 1 cup baby carrots
- 1/4 cup hummus
- 1 tablespoon pumpkin seeds (optional)

Instructions:

1. Arrange baby carrots on a plate with hummus in the center for dipping.
2. Sprinkle pumpkin seeds over the hummus for added texture and nutrients.

Nutritional Facts (per serving):

Calories: 180
Protein: 6g
Carbs: 22g
Fat: 8g

Key Nutrients:

Beta-carotene (carrots)
Zinc (pumpkin seeds)
Fiber (hummus)

Tips:
Swap baby carrots for cucumber slices or bell pepper strips for a crunchy variation.

10. Coconut Bliss Energy Balls

Coconut provides medium-chain triglycerides (MCTs) for energy, while dates offer natural sweetness and magnesium, which supports hormone health.

Prep Time: 10 minutes
Cooking Time: None
Servings: 12 (bite-sized)

Ingredients:

- 1 cup shredded coconut (unsweetened)
- 1/2 cup Medjool dates, pitted
- 1/4 cup almond butter
- 1 tablespoon chia seeds
- 1 tablespoon coconut oil
- 1/2 teaspoon vanilla extract

Instructions:

1. In a food processor, blend all ingredients until a sticky dough forms.
2. Roll the mixture into bite-sized balls and refrigerate for at least 30 minutes.
3. Store in an airtight container in the fridge for up to one week.

Nutritional Facts (per ball):

Calories: 110
Protein: 2g
Carbs: 10g
Fat: 7g

Key Nutrients:

Healthy fats (coconut, almond butter)
Magnesium (dates)
Omega-3s (chia seeds)

Tips:
Roll the energy balls in additional shredded coconut for a beautiful presentation.

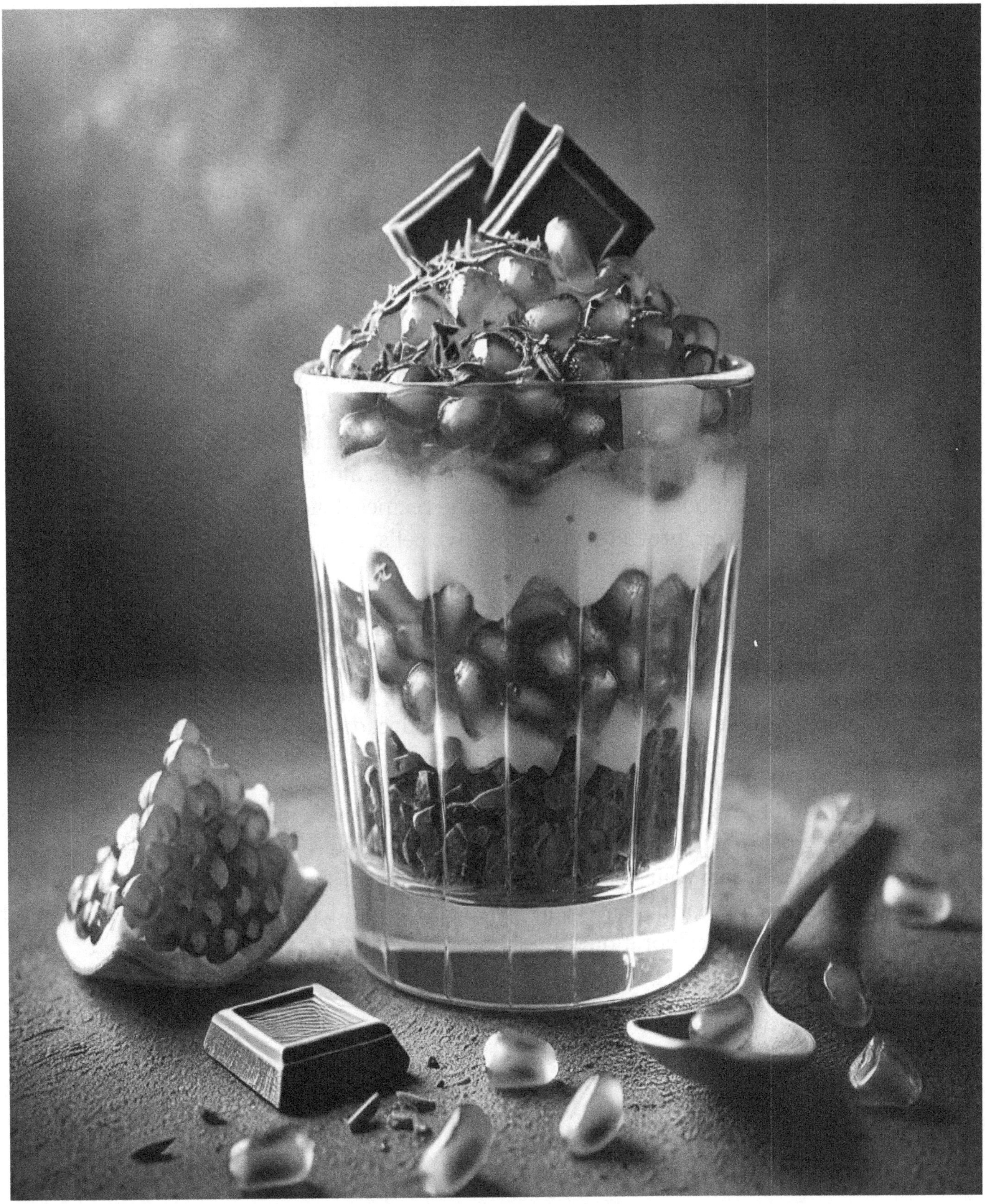

Chapter 7 Desserts and Treats

Everyone loves a little something sweet, but typical desserts often come with a heavy dose of sugar, refined carbohydrates, and unhealthy fats—ingredients that can undermine your fertility journey. While indulgence is a natural and enjoyable part of life, it doesn't have to come at the expense of your health or your goals. This section offers a collection of desserts and treats that allow you to enjoy the sweeter side of life without compromising your commitment to nourishing your body.

Each recipe in this chapter is thoughtfully designed to satisfy your cravings while supporting reproductive health. Instead of empty calories, these desserts are crafted with whole, nutrient-dense ingredients like antioxidant-rich dark chocolate, nuts packed with healthy fats, and fruits that provide natural sweetness along with essential vitamins and minerals. These components not only make the recipes delicious but also contribute to reducing inflammation, protecting reproductive cells, and enhancing hormonal balance.

From creamy avocado mousse to no-bake almond butter fudge, these treats are perfect for sharing or savoring on your own. Many of the recipes also include ingredients like chia seeds, rich in omega-3s, or coconut, known for its healthy fats, making each bite not only indulgent but also beneficial for your body. Whether you're looking for a light and refreshing option like berry coconut ice pops or a decadent choice like almond flour chocolate chip cookies, there's something here to satisfy every sweet tooth.

Desserts should be about joy and enjoyment, and with these fertility-friendly recipes, you can indulge guilt-free. By making intentional choices, you're transforming dessert into an opportunity to nourish your body and bring a little extra sweetness to your fertility journey. These recipes prove that healthy can still mean delicious, turning every treat into a moment of care and celebration.

1. Fertility-Boosting Berry Crumble

Rich in antioxidants, berries help protect eggs and sperm from oxidative stress. Almond flour and flaxseeds provide essential omega-3s and healthy fats for hormonal health.

Prep Time: 10 minutes
Cooking Time: 25 minutes
Servings: 4

Ingredients:

- 2 cups mixed berries (blueberries, raspberries, blackberries)
- 2 tablespoons honey or maple syrup
- 1 teaspoon vanilla extract
- 1/2 cup almond flour
- 1/2 cup rolled oats
- 2 tablespoons ground flaxseeds
- 2 tablespoons coconut oil, melted
- Pinch of cinnamon

Instructions:

1. Preheat the oven to 375°F (190°C) and lightly grease a small baking dish.
2. Toss the berries with honey and vanilla extract, then spread them evenly in the baking dish.
3. In a separate bowl, mix almond flour, oats, flaxseeds, coconut oil, and cinnamon until crumbly.
4. Sprinkle the crumble mixture evenly over the berries.
5. Bake for 20–25 minutes until the topping is golden and the berries are bubbling.
6. Serve warm, optionally with a dollop of Greek yogurt.

Nutritional Facts (per serving):

Calories: 220
Protein: 5g
Carbs: 30g
Fat: 10g

Key Nutrients:

Antioxidants (berries)
Omega-3s (flaxseeds)
Vitamin E (almond flour)

Tips:
For added crunch, sprinkle chopped nuts over the crumble topping before baking.

2. Pomegranate and Dark Chocolate Parfaits

Pomegranates improve blood flow to reproductive organs, and dark chocolate provides antioxidants that protect reproductive cells.

Prep Time: 5 minutes
Cooking Time: None
Servings: 2

Ingredients:

- 1/2 cup pomegranate seeds
- 1/2 cup Greek yogurt (or coconut yogurt for dairy-free)
- 1 tablespoon dark chocolate, grated (70% cocoa or higher)
- 1 teaspoon honey or maple syrup

Instructions:

1. In a serving glass, layer pomegranate seeds, yogurt, and honey. Repeat until the glass is full.
2. Sprinkle grated dark chocolate on top for a decadent finish.
3. Chill for 10 minutes before serving.

Nutritional Facts (per serving):

Calories: 180
Protein: 8g
Carbs: 22g
Fat: 6g

Key Nutrients:

Antioxidants (pomegranate, dark chocolate)
Protein (Greek yogurt)
Calcium (yogurt)

Tips:
Use raspberries or blueberries if pomegranates aren't in season.

3. Cinnamon-Spiced Pears with Walnuts

Pears are a natural source of fiber, helping regulate hormones, while walnuts offer omega-3s to reduce inflammation and support egg and sperm health.

Prep Time: 5 minutes
Cooking Time: 25 minutes
Servings: 4

Ingredients:

- 2 ripe pears, halved and cored
- 2 tablespoons honey
- 1/2 teaspoon cinnamon
- 1/4 cup chopped walnuts

Instructions:

1. Preheat the oven to 375°F (190°C). Place pear halves in a baking dish.
2. Drizzle honey over the pears and sprinkle with cinnamon.
3. Bake for 20–25 minutes, until the pears are tender.
4. Top with chopped walnuts before serving.

Nutritional Facts (per serving):

Calories: 180
Protein: 2g
Carbs: 28g
Fat: 8g

Key Nutrients:

Fiber (pears)
Omega-3s (walnuts)
Antioxidants (cinnamon)

Tips:
Serve with a dollop of plain yogurt for a creamy contrast.

4. Chilled Mango and Lime Sorbet

Mango is rich in vitamin C, supporting egg quality and reducing oxidative stress. Lime adds an extra antioxidant boost.

Prep Time: 5 minutes
Cooking Time: 1 hour (to freeze)
Servings: 4

Ingredients:

- 2 cups frozen mango chunks
- Juice of 1 lime
- 1 tablespoon honey (optional)
- 1/4 cup coconut water

Instructions:

1. In a blender, combine frozen mango, lime juice, honey, and coconut water. Blend until smooth.
2. Transfer to a container and freeze for 1–2 hours for a firmer texture.
3. Scoop into bowls and serve with lime zest if desired.

Nutritional Facts (per serving):

Calories: 120
Protein: 1g
Carbs: 30g
Fat: 0g

Key Nutrients:

Vitamin C (mango, lime)
Hydration (coconut water)

Tips:
Add a pinch of chili powder for a spicy twist.

5. Baked Figs with Almond Drizzle

Figs are rich in magnesium and fiber, promoting hormone balance. Almond butter adds vitamin E, essential for reproductive health.

Prep Time: 5 minutes
Cooking Time: 10 minutes
Servings: 4

Ingredients:

- 4 fresh figs, halved
- 2 tablespoons almond butter
- 1 tablespoon honey
- 1 teaspoon vanilla extract
- 1/4 cup slivered almonds

Instructions:

1. Preheat the oven to 375°F (190°C). Arrange the fig halves on a baking sheet.
2. In a small bowl, mix almond butter, honey, and vanilla until smooth.
3. Drizzle the almond butter mixture over the figs and sprinkle with slivered almonds.
4. Bake for 10–12 minutes, until the figs are soft and fragrant.

Nutritional Facts (per serving):

Calories: 140
Protein: 3g
Carbs: 18g
Fat: 7g

Key Nutrients:

Magnesium (figs)
Vitamin E (almonds)
Fiber (figs)

Tips:
Serve with a sprinkle of cinnamon or nutmeg for added warmth.

6. Orange and Yogurt Honey Tart

Oranges are loaded with vitamin C, which improves blood flow to reproductive organs and supports overall reproductive health. Greek yogurt adds probiotics and protein for hormonal balance.

Prep Time: 10 minutes
Cooking Time: 2 hours (chilling time)
Servings: 8

Ingredients:

- 1 cup Greek yogurt
- 1/4 cup honey
- Zest of 1 orange
- 1 premade graham cracker crust
- Sliced orange segments for topping

Instructions:

1. In a mixing bowl, combine Greek yogurt, honey, and orange zest. Stir until smooth and well combined.
2. Pour the mixture into the graham cracker crust and spread evenly.
3. Refrigerate the tart for at least 2 hours to allow it to set.
4. Just before serving, top with fresh orange segments for a vibrant and refreshing garnish.

Nutritional Facts (per serving):

Calories: 220
Protein: 7g
Carbs: 30g
Fat: 8g

Key Nutrients:

Vitamin C (oranges)
Protein (yogurt)
Probiotics (Greek yogurt)

Tips:
For added flavor, sprinkle a small pinch of cinnamon or nutmeg on top of the tart before serving.

7. Vanilla and Chia Pudding with Passion Fruit

Chia seeds are rich in omega-3s and fiber, which promote hormone health and reduce inflammation. Passion fruit provides vitamin C to protect reproductive cells from oxidative stress.

Prep Time: 5 minutes
Cooking Time: 4 hours (refrigeration)
Servings: 4

Ingredients:

- 1/4 cup chia seeds
- 1 cup unsweetened almond milk
- 1 teaspoon vanilla extract
- 1 tablespoon maple syrup
- 2 passion fruits, halved

Instructions:

1. In a bowl, whisk together chia seeds, almond milk, vanilla extract, and maple syrup. Stir until well mixed.
2. Cover and refrigerate for at least 4 hours or overnight until the mixture thickens into a pudding-like consistency.
3. Spoon the chia pudding into serving glasses or bowls and top with the pulp from the passion fruits.
4. Serve chilled for a refreshing, nutrient-packed dessert.

Nutritional Facts (per serving):

Calories: 220
Protein: 6g
Carbs: 28g
Fat: 10g

Key Nutrients:

Omega-3s (chia seeds)
Vitamin C (passion fruit)
Fiber (chia seeds)

Tips:
For extra sweetness, drizzle a bit of honey or add sliced kiwi on top.

8. Roasted Apple Slices with Cinnamon Yogurt

Apples are high in antioxidants and fiber, which aid hormone regulation and overall reproductive health. Greek yogurt provides probiotics to support gut and hormone balance.

Prep Time: 5 minutes
Cooking Time: 20 minutes
Servings: 4

Ingredients:

- 2 medium apples, cored and sliced
- 1 teaspoon cinnamon
- 1 tablespoon honey
- 1/2 cup Greek yogurt
- 1 teaspoon vanilla extract

Instructions:

1. Preheat the oven to 375°F (190°C). Line a baking sheet with parchment paper.
2. Place apple slices on the baking sheet and drizzle with honey. Sprinkle cinnamon evenly over the slices.
3. Roast for 15–20 minutes, until the apples are tender and slightly caramelized.
4. In a small bowl, mix Greek yogurt with vanilla extract.
5. Serve the roasted apples warm, topped with the cinnamon yogurt.

Nutritional Facts (per serving):

Calories: 180
Protein: 5g
Carbs: 36g
Fat: 2g

Key Nutrients:

Antioxidants (apples, cinnamon)
Probiotics (Greek yogurt)
Fiber (apples)

Tips:
For a crunchy topping, sprinkle crushed walnuts or granola on the apples before serving.

9. Pineapple Coconut Bliss Bites

Pineapple contains bromelain, which supports implantation and reduces inflammation. Coconut provides healthy fats that are essential for hormone production.

Prep Time: 10 minutes
Cooking Time: 30 minutes (refrigeration)
Servings: 12

Ingredients:

- 1 cup shredded unsweetened coconut
- 1/2 cup dried pineapple, finely chopped
- 1/4 cup almond flour
- 1/4 cup coconut oil, melted
- 1 tablespoon honey

Instructions:

1. In a mixing bowl, combine shredded coconut, dried pineapple, almond flour, coconut oil, and honey. Stir until the mixture forms a sticky dough.
2. Roll the mixture into bite-sized balls with your hands.
3. Place the bites on a tray and refrigerate for at least 30 minutes to firm up.
4. Store in an airtight container in the fridge for up to a week.

Nutritional Facts (per bite):

Calories: 110
Protein: 2g
Carbs: 8g
Fat: 9g

Key Nutrients:

Bromelain (pineapple)
Healthy fats (coconut)
Vitamin E (almond flour)

Tips:
Roll the bites in extra shredded coconut for a decorative touch.

10. Avocado and Lime Cheesecake Bars (No-Bake)

Avocado provides monounsaturated fats for hormone health, while lime adds a refreshing dose of antioxidants to protect reproductive cells.

Prep Time: 15 minutes
Cooking Time: 2 hours (chilling)
Servings: 9

Ingredients:

- 1 cup crushed graham crackers
- 2 tablespoons coconut oil, melted
- 2 ripe avocados
- 1/4 cup lime juice
- 1/4 cup honey
- 1/2 cup cream cheese (or dairy-free alternative)
- Zest of 1 lime

Instructions:

1. In a bowl, mix crushed graham crackers with melted coconut oil. Press the mixture firmly into the base of a parchment-lined square pan to form the crust. Refrigerate for 10 minutes.
2. In a blender, combine avocados, lime juice, honey, cream cheese, and lime zest. Blend until smooth and creamy.
3. Pour the avocado mixture over the prepared crust and spread evenly.
4. Refrigerate for at least 2 hours to allow the cheesecake to set.
5. Slice into bars and serve chilled.

Nutritional Facts (per bar):

Calories: 250
Protein: 4g
Carbs: 24g
Fat: 16g

Key Nutrients:

Healthy fats (avocado)
Antioxidants (lime)
Vitamin E (avocado)

Tips:
Top with shredded coconut or a sprinkle of lime zest for added flavor and presentation.

Chapter 8 Supplementing Nutrition with Lifestyle

Lifestyle Factors That Influence Fertility

Fertility is not an isolated function of the body but a reflection of overall health and balance. Nutrition serves as the essential foundation, but it's the lifestyle factors—like exercise, stress management, and sleep—that cultivate an environment where optimal reproductive health can truly flourish. The interplay of these aspects is essential for regulating hormones, enhancing circulation, and minimizing inflammation. This chapter delves into the ways these factors influence fertility and how to make impactful changes to enhance their advantages.

The Role of Exercise in Fertility: Moving Toward Balance

Exercise is frequently highlighted as a fundamental aspect of health, yet in the context of fertility, the specific type, intensity, and regularity of physical activity are vital factors to consider. Engaging in moderate, regular exercise can significantly boost fertility by enhancing blood circulation to the reproductive organs, balancing hormones, and lowering insulin resistance. Nonetheless, it's important to find a careful equilibrium. Engaging in excessive exercise or high-intensity training can lead to hormonal imbalances, which may adversely impact ovulation and the quality of sperm.

For Women

For women, engaging in moderate exercise can play a significant role in regulating the menstrual cycle by helping to balance important reproductive hormones like estrogen and progesterone. Polycystic ovary syndrome (PCOS) is a condition that can affect fertility, and it is frequently associated with insulin resistance. Moderate aerobic activities such as walking, swimming, or cycling can improve insulin sensitivity and support ovulatory function. Additionally, engaging in weight-bearing exercises such as yoga or Pilates can significantly improve circulation to the pelvic area, ensuring that the ovaries and uterus receive a consistent flow of oxygen and nutrients.

For Men

In men, regular exercise promotes testosterone production and reduces oxidative stress, which can damage sperm. Engaging in activities that promote cardiovascular health, like jogging or cycling, can significantly increase blood flow to the testes, which in turn enhances both sperm production and motility. Conversely, engaging in excessive exercise, particularly endurance activities such as marathon running, may lead to a decrease in testosterone levels and an increase in cortisol, that can adversely impact sperm health.

It's important to engage in activities that enhance wellness while being mindful not to strain the body. The American College of Obstetricians and Gynecologists suggests aiming for 150 minutes of moderate aerobic activity each week, which breaks down to roughly 30 minutes a day, five days a week. Yoga and tai chi can be especially helpful for fertility because they blend gentle movement with stress relief, providing a dual advantage for the reproductive system.

Stress Reduction: Easing the Mind, Supporting the Body

Stress is a frequently overlooked yet crucial element that can impact fertility. Chronic stress triggers a series of physiological reactions that can negatively affect reproduction. When the body is consistently in a "fight or flight" mode, it reallocates resources away from non-essential functions, such as reproduction, because it prioritizes survival above all else.

Stress hormones, such as cortisol, can significantly disturb the intricate balance of reproductive hormones. For women, experiencing chronic stress can result in irregular menstrual cycles or even anovulation, which is the absence of ovulation. In men, it may lead to lower testosterone levels, hinder sperm production, and elevate oxidative damage to sperm DNA. Additionally, stress can result in unhealthy coping strategies such as poor eating habits, disrupted sleep, and increased alcohol consumption, all of which can exacerbate fertility issues.

To combat stress effectively, it's essential to engage the parasympathetic nervous system, often referred to as the "rest and digest" mode. Practicing techniques like deep breathing, mindfulness, and progressive muscle relaxation can effectively reduce cortisol levels, fostering a calm state that supports reproductive health. Just dedicating ten minutes a day to focused breathing exercises can lead to noticeable decreases in stress levels.

One of the easiest and most impactful methods for managing stress is by incorporating mindfulness-based practices into your routine. Mindfulness meditation, a practice that encourages individuals to focus on the present moment without judgment, has demonstrated its ability to alleviate anxiety and enhance emotional well-being for couples facing the challenges of infertility. Guided imagery exercises, which involve visualizing positive outcomes or soothing scenarios, can serve as effective tools. For couples, participating in shared activities like hiking, dancing, or cooking together can strengthen their bond and help reduce stress.

Moreover, creating a support network is essential. Connecting with a fertility-focused support group or consulting a therapist who specializes in reproductive health can offer a valuable space to share emotional challenges and gain effective strategies for navigating this journey.

Sleep: The Overlooked Pillar of Fertility

When life becomes hectic, sleep is frequently the first thing we let go, yet its importance for fertility is truly profound. Getting restorative sleep is vital for maintaining hormone balance, supporting cellular repair, and ensuring overall reproductive health. Chronic sleep deprivation can significantly disrupt the body's natural circadian rhythms, which play a crucial role in regulating the release of important fertility hormones like follicle-stimulating hormone (FSH) and luteinizing hormone (LH).

Sleep deprivation can significantly impact women's health, leading to irregular menstrual cycles, decreased egg quality, and challenges with implantation. Inadequate sleep can significantly interfere with the release of gonadotropin-releasing hormone (GnRH), a hormone that helps regulate the menstrual cycle and ovulation. In men, insufficient sleep can lead to a decrease in testosterone levels, which play a vital role in sperm production and motility. Research indicates that men who sleep less than six hours each night experience notably lower sperm counts than those who enjoy seven to eight hours of rest.

Creating a sleep environment and routine that fosters deep, uninterrupted rest is essential for overall well-being. Begin by establishing a regular sleep routine, ensuring you go to bed and wake up at the same time every day, including weekends. It's a good idea to steer clear of electronic devices that emit blue light for at least an hour before you head to bed. This can help ensure that your melatonin production isn't disrupted, promoting a better night's sleep. Melatonin serves as more than just a sleep hormone; it also acts as a potent antioxidant, safeguarding both eggs and sperm from oxidative stress.

Think about incorporating a pre-sleep ritual to help your body recognize that it's time to relax and prepare for rest. Engaging in light stretching, enjoying a good book, or savoring a warm cup of caffeine-free tea, such as chamomile, can be wonderfully soothing and help create a sense of calm. For those facing challenges with insomnia or irregular sleep patterns, exploring options like cognitive-behavioral therapy for insomnia (CBT-I) or acupuncture can provide valuable non-drug approaches to enhance sleep quality.

The Role of Naps

Although getting consistent sleep at night is the best scenario, taking strategic naps during the day can be a helpful way to make up for any sleep shortages. A quick 20-30-minute nap can rejuvenate your body while ensuring your nighttime sleep remains undisturbed. Naps can be especially beneficial for those experiencing stress-related fatigue, as they have the ability to reset the nervous system and enhance focus.

Integrating Exercise, Stress Reduction, and Sleep into Daily Life

These lifestyle factors are beautifully interconnected, so even small changes in one area can have a positive impact on the others. For example, engaging in regular exercise enhances circulation and hormonal balance, while also reducing stress and fostering improved sleep quality. In a similar vein, engaging in stress reduction practices can help lower cortisol levels, which can make it easier for you to both fall asleep and maintain a restful sleep throughout the night.

Start by assessing your current lifestyle and identifying areas for improvement. If exercise seems overwhelming, start with brief, achievable sessions, such as a 15-minute walk after dinner. When stress feels like a constant presence in your life, consider taking just five minutes each morning to engage in deep breathing or mindfulness. This small practice can make a significant difference in how you approach your day. To enhance your sleep, it's important to establish a soothing bedtime routine and consider any environmental elements, like noise or light, that could be interfering with your ability to rest well.

It's important to keep in mind that these changes can be approached gradually and don't have to feel daunting or occur all at once. Even small changes can lead to meaningful improvements in your fertility and overall well-being.

Chapter 9 Additional Resources

Tracking Fertility

Monitoring fertility plays a vital role in contemporary reproductive planning. Recent technological advancements have significantly changed how couples navigate the journey of conception. With the availability of various tools and apps, they can now monitor ovulation cycles, basal body temperature, hormone levels, and much more with remarkable precision. These resources empower individuals with valuable information about their bodies, helping to cultivate a sense of control and awareness during what can often be an uncertain journey. For couples on the journey to conceive, fertility tracking acts as a helpful companion, highlighting the best times for conception while providing valuable insights into overall reproductive health.

Understanding the Science of Fertility Tracking

Fertility tracking fundamentally revolves around gaining insight into the menstrual cycle. Most cycles can be divided into three phases: the follicular phase, ovulation, and the luteal phase. Ovulation marks a crucial moment for conception. It's important to note that the egg remains viable for only about 12 to 24 hours. It's fascinating to note that sperm can actually survive in the female reproductive tract for up to five days. This creates a "fertile window" of about six days during each cycle, which is an important aspect to understand when considering fertility. Recognizing this window is essential for effective fertility tracking.

Key indicators of fertility encompass basal body temperature (BBT), changes in cervical mucus, and surges in luteinizing hormone (LH). After ovulation, BBT experiences a slight increase due to the rise in progesterone levels. During the fertile window, cervical mucus transforms to a clear, stretchy, and egg-white-like consistency, which facilitates sperm movement effectively. LH surges play a key role in triggering ovulation and can be easily detected using urine-based ovulation predictor kits (OPKs). By bringing together these indicators, couples can gain a clearer understanding of their cycle, allowing them to identify their most fertile days with greater accuracy.

Utilizing Technology: Resources and Applications

The emergence of fertility tracking apps and devices has transformed how people keep an eye on their reproductive health. These tools provide intuitive interfaces, automated data analysis, and tailored insights, making them essential for couples on their journey to conceive.

Applications such as Clue, Flo, and Ovia Fertility provide users with the ability to log their symptoms, monitor their cycles, and gain insights into ovulation predictions. They offer helpful reminders for taking temperature readings, recording cervical mucus observations, or using ovulation tests. Numerous apps provide valuable educational content, sharing insights on cycle irregularities, hormone fluctuations, and lifestyle changes that can enhance fertility.

Wearable devices like Ava and Tempdrop elevate fertility tracking by consistently monitoring important physiological markers, including skin temperature, resting heart rate, and breathing rate. These devices connect seamlessly with companion apps, providing real-time data and alleviating the hassle of manual tracking. For those who appreciate a more hands-off approach, these tools can be especially advantageous.

Digital ovulation kits, such as Clearblue, seamlessly integrate traditional urine-based LH tests with user-friendly digital displays, making it easier to understand your results without the uncertainty of interpreting faint lines. Certain advanced models can even assess estrogen levels, offering a more comprehensive view of fertility. If you're looking for greater accuracy, at-home hormone testing kits such as Modern Fertility or Mira can be incredibly helpful. They monitor estrogen and LH levels over time, providing you with valuable insights into your hormone patterns.

Although technology has significantly improved the accessibility and accuracy of fertility tracking, it's important to view these tools as helpful aids rather than absolute solutions. The human body is intricate, and various factors such as stress or illness can lead to fluctuations in cycles. Tracking offers important insights, yet it's essential to also listen to your intuition and stay in tune with your body's signals.

Incorporating Fertility Tracking into Your Everyday Routine

Staying consistent is essential for effective fertility tracking. For instance, measuring BBT involves taking your temperature at the same time each morning, right before you get out of bed. Similarly, cervical mucus observations should be recorded daily for the most accurate patterns. Incorporating apps or devices can certainly enhance these routines, but truly embedding them into your daily habits is what guarantees their reliability.

Involving both partners in the tracking process is essential. Even if one partner takes on the task of logging data or interpreting results, maintaining open communication allows both individuals to feel equally involved in the journey. When partners share the responsibility, it can enhance their emotional connection, transforming tracking into a joint endeavor instead of a lonely chore.

I'm here to help you with whatever you need. Please feel free to share your thoughts or questions, and I'll do my best to assist you. Your concerns are important, and I'm ready to listen and provide support.

When to Seek Professional Advice

Fertility tracking tools and apps can provide valuable insights, but it's important to remember that they should not replace professional medical advice. For couples facing challenges or uncertainties on their conception journey, understanding when to reach out to a healthcare provider is essential. Early intervention helps recognize potential challenges, bring clarity to situations, and present tailored solutions that resonate with personal needs and aspirations.

Identifying the Indicators of Fertility Issues

The timeline for seeking professional advice can differ based on individual age and health history. For women under 35, it's usually advised to reach out to a healthcare provider if you've been trying to conceive for a year without success. Your health and well-being are important, and seeking guidance can provide valuable support on your journey. For women over 35, this timeline is reduced to six months, reflecting the natural changes in egg quality and quantity that occur with age. If either partner has existing medical conditions that may impact fertility, like polycystic ovary syndrome (PCOS), endometriosis, or a past testicular injury, it's wise to seek guidance sooner rather than later.

Common signs that warrant professional evaluation include irregular or absent menstrual cycles, severe menstrual pain, recurrent miscarriages, or difficulty maintaining an erection or ejaculation in men. These symptoms could suggest deeper concerns that might need medical evaluation, including hormonal imbalances, structural abnormalities, or genetic influences.

Even without these signs, couples might find it beneficial to reach out to a provider for reassurance or to undergo a thorough fertility assessment. Fertility testing offers essential insights into ovarian reserve, sperm quality, and reproductive anatomy, empowering couples to make thoughtful decisions about their future steps.

What to Expect During a Fertility Consultation

A fertility consultation usually starts with a thorough review of the medical history for both partners. This includes discussing menstrual cycles, sexual health, lifestyle factors, and any past pregnancies or medical conditions that may be relevant. Next, diagnostic tests are conducted to specifically address the couple's individual circumstances.

Women often undergo several important tests, including bloodwork to check hormone levels like follicle-stimulating hormone, estradiol, and anti-Müllerian hormone. Ultrasound imaging is used to evaluate ovarian reserve and uterine health, while hysterosalpingography (HSG) helps assess the patency of the fallopian tubes. Men typically undergo semen analysis, which examines sperm count, motility, and morphology. Depending on the results, additional tests or referrals to specialists may be recommended.

The goal of these evaluations is not only to identify potential barriers to conception but also to create a personalized plan that aligns with the couple's goals. Treatment options may range from lifestyle modifications and timed intercourse to medical interventions such as ovulation induction, intrauterine insemination (IUI), or in vitro fertilization (IVF).

The Emotional Aspect of Seeking Professional Help

Deciding to seek professional advice can be an emotional milestone, often accompanied by feelings of fear, frustration, or inadequacy. It's important to approach this step with a sense of curiosity rather than self-judgment. Seeking help is a proactive choice, a way of taking control of your journey and accessing resources that can make a difference.

Building a supportive relationship with your healthcare provider is essential. Look for a practitioner who listens to your concerns, explains options clearly, and respects your preferences and values. If you feel dismissed or unsupported, don't hesitate to seek a second opinion. Fertility care is deeply personal, and finding the right provider can make all the difference in your experience.

Navigating Next Steps: Advocacy and Self-Education

Advocating for yourself is a vital part of the fertility journey. While healthcare providers bring expertise, you are the expert on your own body. Ask questions, seek clarification, and voice your priorities during consultations. Keeping detailed records of your cycles, symptoms, and any treatments or interventions can also enhance communication with your provider.

Self-education is equally important. Understanding the basics of fertility science, treatment options, and potential outcomes empowers you to make informed decisions. However, it's crucial to rely on credible sources, such as peer-reviewed studies, professional organizations (like the American Society for Reproductive Medicine), and trusted healthcare providers. Be cautious of misinformation or unproven claims, which can lead to unnecessary stress or false hope.

Chapter 10 Conclusion

As we wrap up this journey through the world of fertility-boosting foods, let's take a moment to reflect on the powerful role that nutrition and lifestyle play in shaping your path to parenthood. This is more than just a cookbook—it's a guide to transforming the way you nourish your body and approach your fertility journey.

The recipes you've explored in this book are more than delicious meals; they are carefully crafted tools designed to deliver the nutrients your body needs to thrive. From breakfasts that kickstart your day with folate, omega-3s, and antioxidants to dinners that encourage bonding while supporting reproductive health, each recipe represents a step forward. These meals are your daily opportunities to care for your body, balance your hormones, and create an optimal environment for conception. Cooking these dishes isn't just about feeding yourself; it's about fueling your future.

We've also delved into the importance of a holistic approach to fertility. Food is foundational, but it's complemented by mindful lifestyle habits like stress management, regular movement, and restful sleep. Together, they create a symphony of health that strengthens your chances of conception and supports your overall well-being. You are taking control of your fertility in the most proactive way possible—by giving your body the care and attention it deserves.

This journey can be both exhilarating and challenging, but every recipe you prepare, every nutrient you embrace, and every lifestyle adjustment you make is a step in the right direction. It's easy to focus on the destination, but don't overlook the progress you've made along the way. Celebrate each small victory, whether it's discovering a new favorite dish, noticing how energized you feel, or feeling more connected to your partner through shared meals and intentions.

Remember, fertility is a complex process, and there's no one-size-fits-all solution. If challenges arise, don't hesitate to seek professional advice or explore additional resources. The key is to stay flexible and resilient, knowing that you are equipping yourself with the best tools and knowledge to navigate this path.

The recipes in this book aren't just about boosting fertility—they're about laying the foundation for a healthy and joyful future. Whether you're preparing these meals for yourself, your partner, or your future family, you are creating habits and traditions that will nourish not only your body but also your spirit.

Above all, know that you are not alone. Many have walked this road before you and have found success in their own time and way. Trust in the process, trust in your body, and trust in the love that motivates you. The path to parenthood may be winding, but with hope, dedication, and the delicious recipes in this book, you are well on your way to creating a family built on care and intention. Keep going, and know that every effort you make today is shaping the future you dream of.

Appendices

Nutrient Index

1. Folate (Vitamin B9)
- Sources: Leafy greens (spinach, kale), asparagus, broccoli, citrus fruits, beans, lentils, and fortified cereals.
- Benefits for Fertility: Folate supports DNA synthesis and cell division, which are critical during early pregnancy and embryo development. It also enhances egg quality and helps reduce the risk of neural tube defects.

2. Omega-3 Fatty Acids
- Sources: Fatty fish (salmon, mackerel, sardines), flaxseeds, chia seeds, walnuts, and algae-based supplements.
- Benefits for Fertility: Omega-3s reduce inflammation, regulate hormone production, and improve uterine blood flow, enhancing implantation potential. For men, they boost sperm motility and quality.

3. Vitamin D
- Sources: Sunlight exposure, fortified dairy products, fatty fish, egg yolks, and mushrooms.
- Benefits for Fertility: Known as the "sunshine vitamin," vitamin D plays a vital role in reproductive health by regulating hormones and supporting egg quality. It also aids implantation and contributes to sperm production and motility.

4. Zinc
- Sources: Shellfish (oysters), beef, pumpkin seeds, sunflower seeds, chickpeas, and nuts.
- Benefits for Fertility: Zinc is essential for hormone regulation, ovarian function, and egg maturation. In men, it boosts testosterone production and improves sperm count and morphology.

5. Iron
- Sources: Red meat, poultry, spinach, lentils, beans, and fortified cereals.
- Benefits for Fertility: Adequate iron levels prevent anemia and support ovulation. It is particularly important for building a healthy uterine lining and maintaining proper oxygen flow to developing embryos.

6. Antioxidants (Vitamin C, Vitamin E, Selenium)
- Sources:
  - Vitamin C: Citrus fruits, strawberries, kiwi, and bell peppers.
  - Vitamin E: Nuts (almonds, sunflower seeds), avocado, and spinach.
  - Selenium: Brazil nuts, fish, turkey, and whole grains.
- Benefits for Fertility: Antioxidants combat oxidative stress, protecting eggs and sperm from damage. They also improve sperm DNA integrity and egg viability.

7. Choline
- Sources: Eggs (especially yolks), soybeans, cauliflower, and liver.
- Benefits for Fertility: Choline supports fetal brain and spinal cord development. It also improves egg quality and may aid in reducing pregnancy complications.

8. Magnesium
- Sources: Dark leafy greens, nuts (almonds, cashews), seeds (pumpkin, chia), whole grains, and dark chocolate.
- Benefits for Fertility: Magnesium helps regulate blood sugar, reduces stress, and supports healthy uterine contractions during implantation.

9. Fiber
- Sources: Whole grains, legumes, fruits (apples, pears), vegetables, and nuts.
- Benefits for Fertility: Fiber helps eliminate excess hormones like estrogen, supporting hormonal balance. It also maintains gut health, which is closely tied to reproductive health.

10. Beta-Carotene
- Sources: Carrots, sweet potatoes, pumpkins, and red bell peppers.
- Benefits for Fertility: Beta-carotene converts to vitamin A in the body, aiding in ovarian health, cervical mucus production, and immune system support.

Frequently Asked Questions

1. Can diet alone improve fertility?
Diet is a crucial component of fertility, but it works best when combined with a holistic approach, including regular exercise, stress management, and adequate sleep. While proper nutrition cannot resolve all fertility issues, it can optimize conditions for conception.

2. How long does it take for dietary changes to impact fertility?
Nutritional changes generally take about three months to influence egg and sperm quality. This period reflects the time it takes for eggs and sperm to mature fully in response to environmental factors, including diet.

3. Are supplements necessary if I follow a fertility-friendly diet?
A well-balanced fertility diet often provides the necessary nutrients, but some individuals may need supplements, particularly for nutrients like folate, vitamin D, or omega-3s. Always consult a healthcare provider before starting any supplements.

4. Does caffeine affect fertility?
Moderate caffeine consumption (less than 200 mg per day) is generally considered safe. Excessive caffeine, however, has been linked to decreased fertility and an increased risk of miscarriage. Consider reducing caffeine intake if you're trying to conceive.

5. Is a vegetarian or vegan diet suitable for fertility?
Yes, a plant-based diet can support fertility as long as it includes sufficient protein, iron, zinc, omega-3s, and vitamin B12. Fortified foods and supplements may be necessary to meet these needs.

6. Can weight affect fertility?
Yes, both underweight and overweight individuals may experience hormonal imbalances that impact ovulation and sperm production. Maintaining a healthy weight through a balanced diet and exercise is key to optimizing fertility.

7. Are there specific foods that improve male fertility?
Foods rich in zinc, selenium, and antioxidants are particularly beneficial for male fertility. Examples include oysters, Brazil nuts, citrus fruits, dark leafy greens, and fatty fish.

8. Does alcohol consumption affect fertility?
Excessive alcohol intake can impair hormone levels, reduce egg and sperm quality, and disrupt ovulation. If you're trying to conceive, it's advisable to limit or avoid alcohol.

9. How can I naturally balance my hormones?
Focus on a diet rich in whole foods, fiber, and healthy fats. Manage stress through techniques like yoga or meditation and avoid refined sugars and processed foods. Adequate sleep and regular exercise also contribute to hormonal balance.

10. Are there foods I should avoid when trying to conceive?
Avoid trans fats, high-mercury fish (like swordfish and shark), excessive caffeine, and heavily processed foods. These can interfere with hormonal health and reduce reproductive success.

References

1. Chavarro, J. E., Willett, W. C., & Skerrett, P. J. (2007). *The Fertility Diet: Groundbreaking Research Reveals Natural Ways to Boost Ovulation and Improve Your Chances of Getting Pregnant.* McGraw-Hill Education.

2. Gaskins, A. J., & Chavarro, J. E. (2018). "Diet and fertility: A review." *American Journal of Obstetrics and Gynecology*, 218(4), 379-389.

3. Grodstein, F., et al. (1994). "The relation of female infertility to consumption of caffeinated beverages." *American Journal of Epidemiology*, 140(6), 491-498.

4. Johnson, S. (2018). "The role of omega-3 fatty acids in fertility." *Human Reproduction Update*, 24(1), 1-10.

5. Mountjoy, M., et al. (2018). "The role of lifestyle in improving fertility." *The Lancet*, 391(10119), 1402-1410.

6. NHS. (2022). "Diet, weight, and fertility." Retrieved from NHS Fertility Resources.

7. Harvard T.H. Chan School of Public Health. (2023). "Nutrition and Fertility." Retrieved from Harvard Public Health.

8. Zeng, X., et al. (2019). "Folate intake and risk of infertility in women." *Nutrition Journal*, 18(1), 1-8.

9. World Health Organization (WHO). (2023). "Nutrition for Reproductive Health." Retrieved from WHO Resources.

10. Wilcox, A. J., et al. (1999). "Caffeine and delayed conception: A European multicenter study on infertility and subfecundity." *American Journal of Epidemiology*, 150(8), 884-892.

Made in the USA
Monee, IL
25 February 2025